A business novel

# A Return to Strategic Leadership

## Judgment in the Age of AI

Book Two of the Strategic Leadership Series

## Mark Van Sumeren

Health
Industry
Advisor, llc

# PRAISE FOR A RETURN TO STRATEGIC LEADERSHIP: JUDGMENT IN THE AGE OF AI

*Mark Van Sumeren has written a business thriller--a book you can't put down. He has also provided strategies on how to confront AI in today's business world that provide a playbook for success. All business leaders, at any stage of their career should read this book. It will be both enjoyable and incredibly helpful."*

**Nancy M. Schlichting**
**Retired President and CEO, Henry Ford Health System**

*"In the age of AI, the managerial habits we've leaned on for a hundred years are crumbling at the edges. But the principles of leadership — both professional and personal — are about to be magnified a hundred-fold. While there's no clear playbook ahead, Mark Van Sumeren's compelling narrative offers a unique opportunity to reflect on what that pathway could be."*

**Tarun Kapoor, MD, MBA**
**Digital Health and Transformation Leader and Strategist**

*An entertaining take on modern business issues.*

**Joe Gleberman**
**CEO, The Pritzker Organization**

*A brilliant meditation on leadership in the era of AI. Mark captures what every executive must confront: technology may accelerate decisions, but only judgment can guide them."*

**Russ Rudish**
**Principal, Rudish Health**
**Former Deloitte Global Healthcare Leader**

*Mark Van Sumeren's "A Return to Strategic Leadership: Judgment in the Age of AI" contends that AI's power is not a substitute for leadership but a force that must be guided. In order to fix and transform healthcare for coming generations, AI undoubtedly will play a critical role. However, AI will need to be strongly accompanied by leadership that includes curated insight, courageous inquiry, moral clarity, and seasoned professional judgement. This is essential reading for mid-career and executive leaders in this age of AI impacting virtually everything in our healthcare world.*

**Mark D. Dixon, President**
**The Mark Dixon Group, LLC**

*Mark Van Sumeren's perspectives on the role of artificial intelligence in today's rapidly changing business environment offer a compelling and timely read for business leaders. His insights remind us that emerging technologies should not be feared but embraced as catalysts for progress. Mark's voice is both unique and essential—serving as a steady guidepost for those who feel uncertain about the fast-approaching future.*

**Jay Takefman**
**Head of Tactical Investments**
**Beach Point Capital**

*Adopting and managing the risks of Artificial Intelligence" is the most difficult decision leaders are focused on, and the most prevalent governance challenge faced in the boardroom. Success requires leadership and diligence when implementing AI as opportunities are endless and the risks of failure are critical. Mark does a wonderful job highlighting the journey all executive leadership teams will be navigating over the coming months (not years!) as technology and capabilities continue to accelerate.*

**Tim (TJ) Johnson**
**Corporate Board Director, Retired Chief Financial and**
**Administrative Officer, Victoria's Secret**

*A Return to Strategic Leadership is the rare business novel that actually feels urgent in 2025 and may well become the defining leadership parable of the AI era.*
*Mark Van Sumeren has crafted a gripping, beautifully written story that reads like a thriller while quietly rewiring how you think about power, judgment, and the future of work. Through Bill Ellis's high-stakes rescue of a legendary consulting firm on the brink of irrelevance, we watch the real-time collision of artificial intelligence, human courage, and institutional soul. You'll recognize every boardroom, every whispered corridor conversation, and every moment of quiet conviction that decides whether an organization lives or dies.*
*This is not another breathless ode to technology. It is a clear-eyed declaration that AI's true impact will not be speed or scale, but the mirror it holds up to our own complacency, and the rare leaders willing to look straight into it. Part succession drama, part ethical manifesto, and part love letter to disciplined renewal, the book leaves you both inspired and unsettled in exactly the right proportions.*
*If you lead anything—a company, a team, or just your own career—this is the one book that will make you ask the question no algorithm can answer: "When intelligence becomes infinite, what is judgment worth? Do we still have it?"*
*Read it before your competitors do.*

**Kevin von Keyserling**
**CEO, ReadySet Surgical, Co-founder, Key Factor**

*The striking visual imagery and three-dimensional characters pull you into Mark Van Sumeren's second lessons-in-leadership-disguised-as-a-novel. But what remains with me after the last page is turned is the questions of how his teachings apply to the field of healthcare. Will AI be healthcare's salvation, or its downfall? It all depends on the leadership, the courage, and the clarity of those who deploy it.*

**Amy Cohn, PhD**
**Arthur F. Thurnau Professor**
**Department of Industrial and Operations Engineering, University of Michigan**
**Chief Transformation Officer, Michigan Medicine**
**Faculty Director, Center for Healthcare Engineering and Patient Safety**

# A RETURN TO STRATEGIC LEADERSHIP

**A Return to Strategic Leadership**
**Judgment in the Age of AI**

Also in the Strategic Leadership series:
*A Trip to Strategic Leadership*

Mark Van Sumeren
Health Industry Advisor LLC
Ann Arbor, Michigan

Published by Health Industry Advisor LLC
Ann Arbor, Michigan

ISBN 978-0-9977403-3-2

This work includes material generated with the assistance of AI. Throughout the process, I used ChatGPT to draft, edit, and repeatedly refine the manuscript. As an engineer by training, I quickly realized that I could not match the tool's speed—nor, at times, its eloquence. Yet I also discovered what Bill Ellis and Barney-Hamilton learned within these pages: while AI can generate words and ideas at remarkable velocity, it still requires the right questions, human context, and judgment to transform those words into meaning.

Cover design by John LeDuc
Printed in the United States of America

# DEDICATION

To the memory of Ed Hardin, a long-time friend, colleague, client, and competitor.

We lost Ed far too early, but his imprint on the healthcare industry remains to this day. Above anything else, Ed was the most ethical, honest, fair, compassionate, loving, and respectful person I have ever been honored to be around. His approach was grounded in his faith — one he never shied from, nor forced on others. He simply lived it.

I believe that Ed would have approved of how Bill Ellis lived his professional career.

MARK VAN SUMEREN

# Table of Contents

# FORWARD

For most of us, artificial intelligence (or AI) has, in a relatively short space of time, become part of our everyday lives.

AI offers us convenience and speed, from simple questions to complex scenarios. Instead of using a search engine to look through the vast amount of information available to us on the Internet, we can simply ask a question and AI will curate the answer: ask it "how long should I cook my Thanksgiving Turkey" and it will offer step by step instructions in a matter of seconds, instead of providing a list of websites that require the reader to look through and interpret the information themselves. At a more advanced level, AI will create content - written, audio, video – all based on the prompts entered by a user and again generated at no cost in a matter of seconds (much to the consternation of the entertainment industry).

However, despite the speed and convenience, the simple answers or more complex content pieces that AI generates are occasionally flawed, particularly when played out over the long term. Ultimately AI is only as good as the questions being asked of it – while it provides us with short-term convenience, the quality of its output is – at least at the current moment – sometimes questionable, and, in extreme cases, even dangerous.

"A Return to Strategic Leadership – Judgment in the Age of AI" offers us a viewpoint into this dichotomy in the corporate environment. Van Sumeren takes us on a well-paced and insightful journey through the halls of a global Consulting partnership that is struggling to remain relevant in the new age of AI. The story's main protagonist, Bill Ellis, represents the human element; his notebook filled with questions, occasionally suffering from a lack of sleep, his belief in his long-term vision unshakeable, even when faced with material setbacks.

Edward Lang, his nemesis, personifies the machine. Always immaculately presented, with all the information at his fingertips, Lang represents the short-term and transactional rewards that fast and easy answers offer; in this case immediate financial benefit for the partners at the long-term existential cost of the Consultancy itself.

As we follow the twists and turns of this journey, we are forced to ask the same questions of ourselves: how should we make the best use of these transformative capabilities? To what extent should we trust our own judgement over the seeming omniscience of AI? Van Sumeren leaves us with a vision of coexistence where we take the best of both elements to drive a collective step forward; the increasing ubiquity of AI in our daily lives means that each of us will need to ensure we use judgment and trust our own long-term goals to make this becomes a reality.

Jo Seed
Chief Strategy and Growth Officer
LogicSource Inc.

# The Call Back

Snow drifted across Ann Arbor in slow, deliberate spirals, the kind of January snow that he loved as a child and hated as a young parent worried about getting the kids off to school before heading to the office. Thick, wet snowflakes fell from the sky, frosting every limb of the countless oaks and elms that covered most of his five-acre property abutting the exclusive Barton Hills Country Club north of Ann Arbor. The early morning storm had already laid a thick, white layer over his lawn.

Now enjoying his fifth year of "retirement", Bill Ellis gazed out his home office window upon the deepening sheet of white, while slowly sipping from his mug of hot, strong coffee. A creature of habit, he preferred Lavazza's Gran Aroma light roast, steeped for exactly four minutes in his single cup French press. Although only 6:30 in the morning, it was Bill's second cup of the day.

So much for retirement.

His seven grandchildren teased him mercilessly about his still-busy schedule. Only a week ago, Bill informed one, Maddie, that he would miss Grandparents Day at her kindergarten class. The precocious five-year-old lamented, "I thought you were (re-)tired!"

In his family's view, he was failing retirement. In his mind, his 40-hour post-retirement work weeks were far more relaxing than the grueling 60-to-70-hour weeks he'd kept up for thirty years following graduation from his beloved University of Michigan. A ten-year stint as COO, and then CEO of the Fortune 300 cardiology device manufacturer, Stone Medical, followed a fast-track career at the blue blood consulting firm, Barney-Hamilton & Co. Both jobs demanded long, stressful hours and aged him beyond his 62 years. The grind also kept him from what he loved most, his family, and the University of Michigan.

He cherished his retirement lifestyle.

His dramatic exit from Stone Medical stunned nearly everyone: the Stone family who founded the business, most of the 5,000 Stone teammates, and its key customers, including the most prominent cardiac surgeons and several of the leading academic medical centers in the country – NYU Langone, the Cleveland Clinic, Mayo, and Cedars-Sinai. Even his family was surprised by Bill's decision to step away in 2021.

Yet, Bill was ready and believed the time was right.

Midway through Bill's tenure at Stone, he rescued the company from an existential crisis, one he'd helped create, if he was honest. Stone had become complacent, burdened by a culture of entitlement which rooted in decades of industry-leading innovation, customer loyalty, and profits that always seemed to climb. Hubris left the company ill-equipped to respond to the succession of shocks that reshaped the healthcare landscape: the 2008 recession, the massive changes that came with the Affordable Care Act in 2010, and a quieter but decisive shift in purchasing power away from physicians and toward margin-hunting health systems. The company lost its market share leadership, its customer service nosedived, and innovation stalled.

The business desperately needed a reset.

That's when Bill launched his now-famous re-invention of Stone Medical. Under his leadership, Vision 2020 set Stone on a path from a struggling manufacturer to an industry innovator. It became case-study material. Harvard wrote about it., McKinsey copied it, and conference organizers practically begged him to retell it.

But Bill had enough.

He stepped away at the peak, convinced that his next chapter would be simpler: teaching part-time at Michigan's Ross Business School, mentoring a few start-ups, maybe giving the occasional keynote on "The Art of Strategic Renewal." His days were filled with books, long walks, and dinners that usually ended before 8 p.m. His phone, mercifully, no longer buzzed through the night. Instead, he became a regular at the Wolverine's home football and basketball games and even showed up for plenty of hockey too. He often traveled with the teams to away games, including the LA Coliseum, the Horseshoe in Columbus, and even that erector-set of a stadium in State College, PA. At home football games, he alternated between his own luxury suite and the President's Suite at the Big House. For basketball games, he usually sat courtside at the Crisler Center, Row 1, directly across from Dusty May and the cagers' bench. From where he sat, every squeak from a pivoting player's high tops pierced your eardrums; beads of sweat from the hustling ballers fell close to your feet. He was that close.

He liked to say he was finally "living on purpose, not urgency."

## A FATEFUL CALL

That peace shattered with one vibration.

His cell phone buzzed on the desk. A familiar number with a New York area code. Although he recognized the number, he almost ignored it. Then curiosity won.

Bill: "Ellis."

Voice: "Bill, it's Robert Gaines."

He froze at the tone of Robert's voice. This was no social call; there was too much strain under the politeness.

Robert Gaines was Chairman of Barney-Hamilton, Bill's old firm. The place where his career had begun, and, in some ways, the place he'd never truly left.

Founded in 1958, Barney-Hamilton built its reputation on restraint. It was never the biggest firm, but it was the one CEOs called when the stakes were existential. Its business wasn't deals or audits; it was

3

judgment. Its counsel shaped industries quietly, without press releases or signatures on the door.

For decades, that discretion was its advantage. But as technology began turning instinct into data and intuition into algorithm, the old firm felt exposed. Independence—the one thing it had always traded on—was now an inefficiency to be priced.

Bill: "Robert. This is a surprise. Are you calling about our upcoming game at Madison Square Garden? I certainly can get tickets for you if you would like to go. St. John's will be tough with Rick Pitino coaching the Red Storm."

Robert: "I wish it were a social call. But it's not. We're in trouble."

Bill sighed softly. "You were always in trouble, Robert. You just hid it better back then."

Robert: "Not this time. The firm's flatlining. Revenues are down, morale's slipping, and innovation's gone quiet. The partnership's fractured. The younger partners want to cash out. The old guard wants to wait it out. And private equity… well, they smell blood."

Bill moved toward the window, looking out over the still accumulating snow.

Bill: "Private equity?"

Robert: "Three serious offers. One from London, one from Chicago, one from Dubai. Big ones. You know, the ones that kick ass, take names, and bury the company in debt. They're circling hard. Some of our partners want to sell."

Bill's grip tightened around his mug.

Robert hesitated. "And there's something else, Bill. Clients are talking about this new AI platform called Erebus. Supposedly, it can simulate a full market-entry strategy in minutes. Financials, competitor matrices, pricing tiers, even risk-weighted scenarios, the kind of work that used to take six weeks and a small army of associates."

Bill frowned. "Erebus?"

"Yeah. Nobody knows much about who built it — rumor is it spun out of a defense analytics lab. But clients are whispering that it's cheaper, faster, and 'never tired.' One of our Fortune 100 clients bragged last week that Erebus gave them a portfolio expansion model over lunch. No consultants involved."

Bill's voice went quiet. "And the partners?"

"Half want to license it. The other half want to sue it. I'm not sure which half scares me more."

Bill turned toward the window, watching snowflakes merge into the glass. "We've competed with arrogance before," he said. "Now we're competing with algorithms."

Robert sighed. "Arrogance never scaled this fast."

He wrote in his notebook four words he didn't love but believed:

*AI eats the middle.*

Robert: "We need leadership, Bill. We need belief."

That word hit him harder than he liked: belief.

Bill: "You've got 600 partners, Robert. Isn't that enough belief for one firm?"

Robert: "Not the kind that counts. We need the kind that changes direction."

A long silence followed.

Bill's gaze drifted to the bookshelf, lined with strategic tomes and leadership memoirs, and to the photo of the 2023 Michigan football team celebrating its national championship. A sea of maize and blue confetti filled the frame. Beneath it, in his own handwriting, he'd written the famous quote (and, Michigan mantra) from Bo Schembechler:

*The team, the team, the team.*

That championship season had meant more to him than most people knew. He had helped build the structure behind the team, the donor consortium that had pioneered Michigan's Name, Image and Likeness (NIL) model, Champions Circle®. It wasn't just philanthropy; it was structure. Leadership in disguise.

Michigan had done what few thought possible: adapt to the new world of NIL without losing its soul. And it worked.

He turned back toward his desk, his mind already shifting into analysis.

Bill: "Send me the financials. And a list of your top twenty clients."

Robert (quietly): "Does that mean you'll come back?"

Bill hesitated. "No. It means I'll take a look."

Robert: "Then look fast. The Management Committee meets Friday. And they're running out of patience."

The call ended.

For a long moment, Bill stood in the stillness. The snow kept falling, indifferent to Bill's inner turmoil and the foreboding urgency of Barney-Hamilton's crisis.

He set his coffee mug down, opened his notebook, and wrote four words across a blank page:

*Legacy without renewal dies.*

He stared at them for a moment, then underlined renewal.

That's when the phone buzzed again, this time, it was a text from Sarah Kim, his former protégé at Stone Medical.

"Heard from Barney-Hamilton yet? Word is, they want you back. Don't do it unless you're ready to break some glass."

He smiled. She knew. She always knew.

## LATER THAT MORNING

He drove into town, tires crunching through the snow, and found himself, as he often did, pulling into the parking lot of Schembechler Hall. The building was quiet in the off-season, but the bronze statue of Bo out front looked as defiant as ever.

Inside, the athletic director, Warde Manuel, greeted him warmly.

Warde: "Bill! Haven't seen you since the championship game in Houston."

Bill: "Just couldn't stay away. Needed a little inspiration."

Warde (laughing): "Then you came to the right place. This program used to think tradition was enough. NIL changed that fast."

Michigan football is soaked in tradition. The program claims 1,012 victories on the gridiron prior to the start of the 2025 season; no other team has even neared the 1,000-win milestone. Their stadium, dubbed "The Big House" by legendary broadcaster Keith Jackson, seats 107,601 fan(atic)s. During every home game, the public address announcer boasts that the stadium hosts,

*The largest crowd attending a game anywhere in America today.*

They have drawn 100,000-plus to every non-Covid home game since 1975.

A recording of none other than the legendary James Earl Jones stirs the home crowd before the team runs under the banner prior to kickoff,

*Welcome to the University of Michigan*

*We are the greatest University in the World!*

*We believe in football. Championship football.*

*We bow to no man. We bow to no program.*

Jones' voice gives the stadium a collective shiver.

Bill and Warde walked down the hall lined with championship banners. Twelve in total dating back to 1901. Each one gleamed, but the newest, 2023, shone with extra polish.

Warde: "This program used to think tradition was enough. NIL changed that fast."

Tradition, Bill thought, wasn't the armor people believed it was. In consulting, as in football, legacy could become an anchor. And somewhere in a glass tower or cloud cluster, he imagined, Erebus — whatever it truly was — was busy disassembling that legacy line by line, teaching clients how to live without them.

He pushed the thought aside, but it lingered, like static you couldn't quite tune out.

At Barney-Hamilton, consultants still worshiped at the altar of intellect, unaware that somewhere in Silicon Valley, an algorithm had begun imitating them with terrifying fluency. Erebus, Robert had said. The name stuck in his head like a song he didn't like but couldn't stop humming.

He pushed the thought away, not yet knowing that the ghost he dismissed would soon walk through his office door.

That night, back at home, Bill poured himself two fingers of Basil-Heyden, neat, and sat at his desk. He reread the numbers Robert had sent. The picture was grim: stagnant revenue, client growth stuck in neutral, and partner withdrawals on the rise.

Barney-Hamilton, once the Harvard of consulting, had drifted into bureaucracy: rich in intellect, not so rich in innovation.

And yet, beneath the data, he saw something else, a pattern of complacency that looked eerily familiar.

He flipped back to the photo of Michigan's championship celebration. The banner read,

*Leaders and Best*

He whispered to himself, "Maybe it's time to lead again."

## TWO DAYS LATER – NEW YORK

Barney-Hamilton occupied the top twenty floors of a fifty-two-story tower, a vertical city of glass and judgment. The building's lobby served dozens of firms, but only one name carried to the skyline.

Bill exited the elevator on the 39th floor, nodded at the receptionist, then let his eyes drift across the wall of portraits, the founders and the rainmakers, the old legends he used to work for. His own photo was there, mid-level, back when he'd been the firm's youngest-ever partner.

He hardly recognized the man in the picture, dark hair, sharp suit, and relentless eyes.

*Let's see if I've got one more turnaround left.*

## INSIDE THE BOARDROOM

The Barney-Hamilton boardroom was a monument to prestige, twenty feet of polished mahogany framed by glass walls and a skyline view of midtown Manhattan. On one wall, a digital dashboard pulsed with key performance indicators:

*Revenue Growth: -1.4%. Client Retention: 72%. Partner Withdrawals: +18%.*

Inside, the Management Committee was already gathered: regional heads, the functional chiefs, plus a long row of practice leads. Twenty-four people in all—the ones who claimed to steer the ship.

Bill stood silently, letting the numbers speak.

Robert Gaines: "That's the picture. Three straight years of flat growth, rising attrition, and no clear differentiator left in our portfolio. We're getting out-thought and out-priced."

Bill: "By whom? The boutiques?"

Robert: "Not exactly. By our own clients."

Bill turned. "Explain."

Robert: "They're doing in-house what they used to hire us for - strategy, operations, even full-blown transformation programs. They're using AI platforms, building them internally or licensing them from tech vendors. Tools that can do in minutes what we used to charge millions for."

He motioned to the screen, where a slide appeared showing a case study:

*Global bank develops proprietary AI to simulate market-entry strategies in 17 minutes, eliminates need for outside consultants.*

Sally Kerns, Partner-in-Charge of the Americas: "That was one of ours. Five years ago, that project billed $25 million. This year, the same client ran the analysis through an AI engine, for less than the cost of our proposal."

Bill exhaled slowly. "So, we've become the middleman between intelligence and execution, and the middle is disappearing."

Robert: "Exactly. Clients are discovering they don't need armies of analysts anymore. They need someone to help them interpret what AI tells them, to make sense of it. But we're still organized to deliver decks, not decisions."

Bill: "What are we doing about it?

James Crowley, CIO: "We've created an 'AI Task Force.' They're benchmarking tools, exploring vendor partnerships…"

Bill raised a hand. "Stop. That's the same thing every complacent firm says before it dies, 'We have a task force.'"

James (defensive): "Bill, it's not that simple. Our reputation…"

Bill: "… is precisely what's blinding us. Reputation doesn't protect you from irrelevance. Ask Kodak. Ask Blockbuster. Ask any company that confused history for immunity."

He began pacing. "You're all describing the symptoms, not the disease. The problem isn't AI, it's that our clients have learned faster than we have. They've democratized insight, and we're still selling exclusivity. Our model was built on the idea that intelligence was scarce. It's not scarce anymore, it's ubiquitous. What's scarce now is judgment."

Silence.

Bill: "Here's the part we never admit out loud. We sold confidence dressed up as clarity. Now the machines can do that too, and cheaper. If we're going to survive, we must redefine our value around what technology can't replicate: context, courage, and conviction."

A few heads nodded. Others looked uncomfortable.

Robert: "That's why we need you, Bill. You see the iceberg before the rest of us."

Bill: "Seeing it isn't the issue, Robert. It's whether you're ready to steer."

He turned to face the group.

Bill: "AI isn't the enemy. It's the mirror.

What he meant, though few yet understood, was that the power of any algorithm was never intrinsic; it was derivative. Its usefulness depended entirely on the discipline of those who used it. Over time, Bill would refer to the Four Factors of Judgment: the quality of the data you feed it, the precision of the questions you ask, the human values that shape how you use it, and the professional expertise you bring when you interpret what it spits back. Take away any one of the four, and you didn't have judgment anymore; you had automation - fast and confident, but hollow.

"We've built a firm so proud of its process," he continued, "that we forgot its purpose."

He gestured toward the screen again. "Strategy isn't about producing faster answers. It's about asking better questions. And right now, machines are out-questioning us."

Sandy Phillips, CHRO (quietly): "So what do we do?"

Bill: "We stop acting like consultants and start thinking like creators. We must turn this firm into a platform, a place where human judgment and machine intelligence combine into something no client can replicate."

Robert: "That's a complete reinvention of our model."

Bill: "Exactly. Anything less, and private equity won't need to buy us, they'll just wait for gravity to finish the job."

## THE VOTE

The boardroom fell into a contemplative quiet.

Robert finally spoke: "Bill, we've danced around it long enough. Will you take the reins again?"

Bill studied their faces. He saw fear, but beneath it, exhaustion. They weren't lazy; they were lost.

He thought of Michigan football again, the moment before the NIL transformation, when the program was paralyzed by its own legacy. The parallels were uncanny: old success models, an incentive system that hadn't kept up, and a world changing faster than its leaders could imagine.

Back then, Michigan hadn't waited to be saved. It had redefined itself.

Bill: "If I take this on, I'll need your full backing. No half-measures, no politics, no sacred cows. We'll have to question everything, from how we price, to how we partner, right down to how we define work itself."

Edward Lang, Global Head of Strategy: "And if we can't stomach that?"

Bill: "Then you should sell now. Because the rest of us will be too busy rebuilding to look back."

Robert nodded, and the partners exchanged glances. Slowly, one by one, hands began to rise.

Robert: "Then it's settled. Bill Ellis returns as Managing Partner of Barney-Hamilton."

A ripple of subdued applause followed, polite, cautious, but tinged with hope.

Bill gave a small nod. "Alright. Let's get to work."

He reached for his notebook and wrote a single line across the top of a clean page:

*If intelligence is everywhere, leadership must become exceptional.*

He snapped the cover shut.

## THE RIDE HOME

That night, as his car crawled toward the Marriott LaGuardia through the winter slush, Bill replayed the meeting in his head. The firm was in deeper trouble than the numbers showed. Its problem wasn't just structural, it was spiritual.

Barney-Hamilton had forgotten how to learn.

Outside, neon lights flickered across rain-streaked windows, an endless stream of color and code, of algorithms humming in unseen networks. In a world where machines could model markets, diagnose diseases, and write symphonies, what did it mean to lead anymore?

Bill didn't know the answer yet, but he knew where to start.

He texted Sarah Kim.

*Looks like I'm back in. AI is eating consulting alive. Time to find what still makes us human.*

She replied almost instantly.

*Good. Because that's the only advantage left.*

## DAWN, ANN ARBOR

By the time Delta flight 1231 touched down at Detroit's Wayne County airport (DTW), the first light of morning glowed faintly over southeastern Michigan. Bill looked out the window as the runway lights blurred beneath him.

He thought of two revolutions, one on the football field, the other in the boardroom, both born from the same truth: you can't outspend disruption; you must outlearn it.

He closed his notebook and whispered to himself,

*Let's win another one.*

Then he stepped out into the Michigan cold, the air sharp, the mission clear.

MARK VAN SUMEREN

CHAPTER 1

# Welcome Back to the Ivory Tower

The taxi let him out on 40th Street with a hiss of brakes and the sour breath of winter riding the exhaust. From the curb, Barney-Hamilton's headquarters rose like a promise the firm kept trying to live up to: fifty-two stories of glass cut clean against a winter-grey sky. Bill Ellis paid the driver, tugged his coat tighter, and crossed into the lobby's heat.

The building knew how to perform. It always had.

When Bill Ellis stepped through Barney-Hamilton's revolving doors at 7:12 a.m., the lobby was the same marble echo chamber Bill remembered from the 1990s, white stone, too many black suits, and a low hum of polite panic. What had once been a temple of intellect now felt like an airport where no one knew their gate.

The partners called it "strategic interest." Bill knew better. When private equity started asking questions, it wasn't curiosity; it was appetite. Ardent Capital had analysts model its value at just under a billion dollars, offering a rich premium for control. "We can help unlock the next phase of your growth," Jonathan Armitage had said on a call that somehow found its way to Bill through a former client. "We're not predators, Bill— we're partners who move fast." Bill knew better than to believe in friendly takeovers.

Bill stepped through the revolving doors into the marble lobby, where a uniformed security officer scanned IDs and issued visitor badges.

"Mr. Ellis, forty-third floor?" the guard asked, glancing at his screen.

"Thirty-nine," Bill corrected.

"Right. Barney-Hamilton reception. Express elevators, bank C."

Bill nodded and crossed the atrium toward the elevator bay, the hum of polished efficiency all around him.

He flashed his badge—someone had reactivated it overnight—and stepped into the elevator. It swallowed him whole and began its frictionless climb. He felt the old sensation without meaning to as the numbers climbed, the air thinned, and the decisions awaiting above him gathered like weather.

# RECEPTION

When the doors opened on thirty-nine, the space changed; quieter, restrained. The reception area that smelled faintly of espresso and varnish. The skyline lay propped against the windows like a painting. Two assistants waited by the glass reception wall, tablets in hand.

"Good morning, Mr. Ellis," one said. "We have your schedule."

Before they could say another word, another elevator opened and a burst of partners poured out—Elena Martínez, head of operations; Tariq Khan, the firm's quietly brilliant data scientist; and Maya Guilett, a Partner in Barney Hamilton's healthcare practice. They stopped mid-stride.

Elena recovered first. "Well, the ghost returns."

"Not a ghost," Bill said. "Just someone who wandered back."

She hugged him, and for a moment the room warmed.

He moved down the hallway, past framed magazine covers trumpeting the firm's greatest hits: Saving the Airline Industry. Reinventing National Health Systems. The rest he barely remembered. His own face appeared on one, fifteen years and several lifetimes ago, beneath a headline that called him "The Reluctant Reformer."

He remembered the interview. He'd told the reporter that transformation rarely failed for lack of ideas; it typically failed for lack of courage.

He wasn't reluctant today.

# PREPARATION

Robert was waiting in the corner office, jacket off, tie loosened. He looked as though he had slept on a plane and argued with a spreadsheet. He looked up and broke into the expression Bill had missed: a smile that was eighty percent relief and twenty percent restraint.

"You're early," Robert said.

"I woke up in the wrong decade," Bill replied. "Figured I'd better walk it off."

Robert's laugh was gravel smoothed by time. He handed Bill a thin folder, no thicker than a menu. "Town hall agenda," he said. "And a seating chart for the dignitaries who don't like to be surprised."

"Anyone ever tell them that's not what a dignitary is for?"

Robert gestured at a low table spread with printouts. "We've got a packed room at nine. Streaming to all offices. Your audience today: three hundred equity partners, another hundred-plus fixed-share partners, a few thousand staff, alumni, and God knows who else sharing the link."

"Everyone's listening," Bill said. "Good."

Robert lowered his voice. "A heads up. You'll get questions about the PE offer. Some want to reopen negotiations. They're calling the last vote 'advisory.' And…" he paused. "Lang is going to test you."

Bill gave a half-smile. "Lang always does."

Robert hesitated, then added, "He's been quoting Erebus in meetings."

"Erebus?"

"The AI platform clients are falling in love with. Some of our healthcare accounts already use it to simulate strategy options. They're bragging about finishing in hours what used to take our teams months."

Bill's expression didn't change, but the thought stuck. "So even the clients are consultants now."

"Cheaper ones," Robert said quietly. "Ones that don't need a bonus pool."

Bill let out a slow breath. "We've built a cathedral, Robert. Now everyone's praying at vending machines."

Robert smiled ruefully. "That's why you're back."

Edward Lang had the kind of résumé that could silence a room. A Wharton MBA, a Rhodes Scholar finalist, and former managing director at the private-equity powerhouse Eclipse Capital. He had joined Barney-Hamilton fifteen years earlier, back when partnership still meant something sacred, and had risen quickly; equal parts brilliance and calculation. Colleagues admired his intellect and feared his timing. Ed spoke in the crisp, unemotional sentences of an analyst who saw people as variables and conviction as an expense. To clients, he was indispensable; to Bill Ellis, he was the embodiment of the firm's existential dilemma, ambitious enough to save Barney-Hamilton, and impatient enough to sell it.

Robert looked at Bill, as if searching his face for doubt. "Anything you need me to say?"

"Just introduce me. Then let me talk to them like grown-ups."

"Every day," Robert's eyes warmed. "You ready?"

"No," Bill said. "But I'm here."

## TOWN HALL

The corridor outside the auditorium was already crowded. Analysts in dark sweaters, managers in careful navy, partners in the uniform of expensively effortless.

The auditorium was half amphitheater, half runway; you could feel the budget in the light rigs and the sound that had heft without volume. Screens bracketed the stage like bookends. At the back, the A/V crew spoke a language made of numbers and shrugging.

When the room filled, its noise resolved into a single presence: the weight of expectation. Thousands more watched on the global feed:

Singapore before midnight, London at tea, São Paulo with late-afternoon sun slanting through blinds.

Robert opened with a stewardship tone. "We're here to speak plainly," he said. "We're here to tell you what we know, and what we don't."

He kept it short. Introduced Bill. Sat down.

When the town-hall lights came up and the room settled, Bill stood at the lectern and let the silence sit on the wood. He did not look at the notes the communications team had sent, bulleted with corporate phrases like alignment and synergy that he never intended to use.

"Good morning," he began. "I'm going to skip the pleasantries. I'm not going to inspire you. I'm going to tell you the truth. You don't need another speech. You need a reason to believe again."

A rustle. He let it pass.

"Here's what's true: we've been flat three years. Partner defections are a symptom, not a cause. And clients—some of the same people who owe us their last five turnarounds—are trying toolkits and platforms that can replicate the analytical engine we spent sixty-eight years perfecting."

He let replicate sit in the air. You could hear the HVAC think.

A throat cleared somewhere in the third row. He didn't look to see who.

"I'm not here to save Barney-Hamilton," he began. "I'm here to remind it what it was built to do."

He walked slowly, scanning faces that ranged from curiosity to calculation. "This firm used to be about judgment. Now it's about throughput. We were the world's best at asking questions; somewhere along the line we decided answers were more billable."

Bill paused, glancing toward the cameras streaming the event.

"Our challenge isn't just private equity. It's that the very idea of expertise is being rewritten. Tools like Erebus are democratizing intelligence, taking what once made us indispensable and making it downloadable. We can't out-compute machines. We can only out-understand them."

Nervous laughter.

"I returned because we have two truths to face at once. The first is internal: our partnership model, the one that built this place, is straining under its own weight. It rewards tenure over contribution, consensus over courage, predictability over imagination. Our partnership model taught me everything I'm to know. However, it now pays people to play last year's game, distributing success faster than we build it. We hide risk by punishing it, then wonder why courage goes quiet.

The second truth Is external: They're using agentic platforms — tools that learn, synthesize, and predict — sometimes better than we do. Our clients are discovering they can do in minutes what we used to charge millions to provide. Intelligence has been democratized. Decks have been commoditized. Confidence is now available on subscription. AI will not make us obsolete—unless we insist on behaving like a deliverable instead of a partner."

He let that sink In. "The consulting industry was built on scarcity — the scarcity of understanding. But the machines have broken that monopoly. If we don't redefine what we sell, Erebus and its cousins will turn our legacy into a library of footnotes."

"What's scarce now is judgment. And the courage to use it."

He could feel the room draw closer.

"If we keep selling answers, we will lose to machines. If we start selling better questions, framed by context and ethics, we will lead the era those machines are enabling. The conviction is the part only we can supply."

Hands moved to chins. Laptops stopped. Even the latecomers hovering in the back stopped hovering.

"I won't pretend this is simple. It isn't. We have habits that feel like values and incentives that look like truths. We've made process into religion. Today, we begin making purpose our practice."

"We face two existential challenges," he continued. "One: private equity thinks it can own us. Two: artificial intelligence thinks it can replace us. Both might be right—if we allow it."

He paused. "But know this to be true: judgment still matters. Maybe more than ever. Our clients don't just want predictions; they want meaning. They want to know which numbers matter."

He reached for a slim folder on the lectern and held it up. "This is our First Thirty Days. It's not a strategy. It's a reset of how we think, decide, and own our future. Five moves."

He opened the folder, reading each line as if pinning it to the room.

"One: A Listening Tour with teeth. Forty client conversations in thirty days with CEOs, CFOs, CHROs, heads of strategy. I will ask each a single question: Where did we stop being useful? We will publish the themes internally, unvarnished."

A rustle. People weren't used to hearing the word unvarnished in this room.

"Two: The Belief Index. We will measure the scarcest resource we have—belief—in three places: clients, people, partners. Not Net Promoter Scores. Not brand surveys. Just belief. Do you believe Barney-Hamilton makes you better? If not, why not?"

He saw a partner in the third row, one of the cynics, tilt his head, interested despite himself.

"Three: Judgment Studios. Cross-disciplinary rooms where teams pair with AI tools to tackle live client problems in real time. Not pilots. Practices. We'll stream some sessions to clients—open kitchen—so they can see how our minds work beside the machines."

A whisper: risky. Another: necessary.

"Four: The Contribution Ledger. Effective next quarter, we begin allocating a portion of partner equity based on contribution: IP created, capability built, clients renewed, talent developed. Tenure still matters. But contribution matters more."

That one landed like a rock dropped into a lake. People shifted in their seats.

"Five: The Sacred Cow Inventory. Every process, ritual, committee, and report that exists because 'we've always done it this way' goes on a list. You will have to justify it by purpose. If it doesn't serve purpose, it goes."

He closed the folder.

Bill waited, letting the air settle after the ripple of murmurs. Then, with the timing of someone who understood theater as much as leadership, he said quietly:

"There's one more move."

The room stilled.

"The move that decides whether we lead this era—or watch it pass."

He clicked the remote. One word filled the screens:

*Agentic*

"The world is chasing AI," Bill said. "But what's coming isn't artificial, it's agentic. Systems that act, reason, and learn on their own loops. Tools that simulate an entire market strategy before your meeting ends."

He paced the stage. "Every firm in our industry is racing to bolt AI onto its processes. They'll all use the same models, trained on the same public data. That means sameness, not strategy. Speed will be free. Judgment won't."

He gestured to the screen again. Four words appeared:

*Public Data / Curated Memory*

"Our clients can buy intelligence anywhere. What they can't buy is our experience. Sixty-eight years of engagements, lessons, and scars that no public dataset can replicate. That's our moat. Not secrecy—curation."

He turned back toward the partners.

"We'll build our own corpus—clean, secure, anonymized—a living library of Barney-Hamilton's collective memory. That becomes the substrate for our agentic tools. Public data gives speed; our Memory gives truth. That's how we'll compete."

He paused. "But machines don't interpret. They don't prioritize. They don't care. That's our work."

New slide:

*Translator / Sense-Maker*

"Two new roles start here. Translators: people who interrogate the agents, stress-test assumptions, and frame the right prompts. Sense-Makers: the veterans who turn the agent's analysis into action, ethics, and consequence. That's where our edge lives."

He smiled faintly. "If you've ever said, 'I wish I had time to think,' congratulations—you're about to. The agents will handle the grunt work. You'll handle the meaning."

A final slide:

*From Hours → Outcomes*

"We stop selling hours. We start pricing outcomes and risk. Clients pay for impact, not time. More for the improbable, less for the obvious. That's how we reprice judgment in an age that automates intelligence."

He stopped speaking. Silence, thick and electric.

"This is how we win," he said finally. "By turning this firm into a platform—human judgment and machine intelligence, fused by Memory and meaning. Models can be rented. Memory and courage cannot."

He looked out across the crowd. "Every other firm will rent intelligence. Only Barney-Hamilton will own the experience—and the courage—to turn it into leadership."

"This is not a stunt. It's a pivot. Strategy follows the habits of attention. We change those first."

A hand went up before he could leave the lectern. Edward Lang didn't wait to be called.

"May I?" Lang said, the microphone catching his politeness like light on glass.

Bill gestured: Please.

"Edward," Bill said, as if inviting an old teammate to take the next rep.

Lang stood, jacket perfectly cut, hair perfectly silver. He didn't raise his voice; he never needed to.

Lang turned to the room, not to Bill. "There are ways to change, and there are ways to perform. Mr. Ellis prefers the former. I prefer the latter. Clients don't need to sit in our kitchen. They need dinner. On time."

Laughter he could pretend was agreement.

"We can modernize without self-immolation," Lang continued. "Private equity is offering us capital, discipline, and relief. We might not like the optics. But optics don't pay salaries. We don't need to turn this place into a therapy group to find a conscience."

A few nods—older, tired. Some eyes reached for the comfort of an earlier, less turbulent era, yet fearful that there may be no return.

Bill let the room re-balance on its own axis. Then he said, "If I ever sell us therapy, fire me. I'm selling us work. Harder work than we've done in years. Work that will hurt—because it matters."

"Bill, eloquence is our native tongue here. We can speak vision with the best of them. But vision doesn't pay the draw. Our associates are already nervous; our partners are watching their capital account like hawks. You're proposing to change the engine mid-flight. Why should anyone trust that we'll land the plane?"

Bill could have answered a dozen ways. He chose the clearest one.

"Because we'll fly it together," he said. "And because the alternative is to keep polishing the tray tables while the wings fall off."

A few laughs. Lang's eyes narrowed but not unkindly.

"And" Bill added, "because we've done this before. Maybe not here, but in places that matter. I've seen a century-old program change its incentive system, its recruiting philosophy, its playbook—and win a national championship without selling its soul. I watched donors stop donating and start building. Coaches stop guarding and start sharing. Players owned their brand without breaking the team."

He let the parallel hang without naming it.

"We don't need to be younger to be faster. We need to be braver to be better."

Lang folded his arms. "One more." He nodded toward the cameras. "Private equity. Are we reopening discussions?"

"No," Bill said. "If we do our work, the question will disappear. If we don't, the answer won't matter."

He didn't raise his voice. "You can take Ardent's money and buy time. Or you can take responsibility and build it. I know which one turns you into an asset and which one makes you an owner."

He stepped back. "Questions?"

A beat. Then a line of hands—real questions now, not tests.

"How will the Contribution Ledger account for enablers, not just rainmakers?"

"By defining contribution to include four currencies: insight, client trust, capability, and culture. If you grow one at the expense of the others, you net to zero."

"What about pricing when AI collapses the hours?"

"We stop selling hours. We price outcomes and risk, not time. We'll create an option-style fee for uncertainty—clients pay less if we deliver the obvious, more if we create the improbable."

"How do we keep our young stars from bolting to tech?"

"By giving them ownership of the things they build here—code, frameworks, communities—and a path to recognition that doesn't take twelve years."

A partner in the back, one Bill didn't know, raised a hand halfway. "And belief? How does one measure belief without turning it into another dashboard we ignore?"

Bill smiled. "You don't measure belief to manage it. You measure it to face it. My experience? Belief is the only metric that tells you, before revenue does, whether the future wants you in it."

Hands, hesitations. A manager in his thirties asked about layoffs. A partner asked if "equity" meant dilution or humiliation. An analyst asked if the Studios would be open to people like her or if she should wait her turn, like always.

"Come to The Lab at five," Bill said, surprising himself naming a room that didn't exist. "We'll start with you."

He closed with what felt like a mistake even as he said it. "I don't need you to believe in me," he told them. "I need you to believe in us. If you can't yet, lend me your doubt. I'll pay interest."

The room exhaled as one organism. Robert returned, took the mic, ending the session with a promise of scheduling and next steps, "We'll publish the Studios sign-up by close of business."

The partners clapped politely, unsure whether they'd been inspired or indicted. Bill could feel the tension—an undercurrent of skepticism humming like electricity.

As people stood, the low roar of conversation rose, the sound of a beehive deciding whether to swarm.

Robert joined Bill at the edge of the stage. "You didn't lose them."

"I didn't try to win them," Bill said. "I tried to tell them the truth."

"You threaded a needle," Robert said.

"I stabbed a balloon," Bill replied. "Let's hope it was the right one."

"Lang will regroup."

"I'm counting on it," Bill said. "I need him as a foil until he becomes a partner."

"He is a partner," Robert said.

"You know what I mean."

When the session ended, people didn't rush the exits the way they usually did. They lingered, forming small circles where they argued gently among themselves. You could tell when a conversation was about to matter when people forgot to look at their watches.

## QUESTIONS AND ANSWERS

By late afternoon, an internal document began circulating through inboxes and chat threads—half rumor, half reassurance. Its title:

*FAQ: The Ellis Plan—What We Know (And What We Don't).*

No one knew who wrote it, though most assumed Bill had quietly approved it. It wasn't marketing copy; it was stripped down, direct, and impossible to misinterpret.

FAQ: THE ELLIS PLAN — WHAT WE KNOW (AND WHAT WE DON'T)

Q: Is Barney-Hamilton becoming an AI company?
A: No. We're becoming a firm that uses agentic intelligence to amplify human judgment. Machines will handle the noise; we'll handle the meaning. AI is the tool. Judgment is the differentiator.

Q: What's the "Memory Project"?
A: Our greatest asset isn't our client list; it's our collective experience. We're curating sixty-eight years of anonymized project data into a clean, structured corpus that captures how Barney-Hamilton thinks, decides, and learns. This curated "Memory" will power our proprietary agentic systems and form the core of our competitive moat.

Q: Are analysts or managers being replaced by Erebus or our own AI?
A: No. But roles are evolving. Automation will erase repetitive analysis and free our people to do the one thing machines can't: interpret with context. If you joined to think, your value will rise. If you joined to format decks, your time is running short.

Q: Why stop selling hours?
A: Because time isn't the product anymore; insight and risk-sharing are. We'll price engagements on outcomes, not effort. This isn't a cost-cutting maneuver; it's an honesty maneuver.

Q: What exactly is the Belief Index?
A: A mirror, not a metric. Once a month, we'll ask three
questions across clients, partners, and staff. The answers will be
public—internally. When belief falls, we ask why. When it rises,
we ask why harder.

Q: How will the Contribution Ledger change compensation?
A: It will link ownership to contribution, not seniority. Equity
will begin to rebalance toward those who build capability,
mentor talent, and renew clients. Expect friction. Expect fairness
earned in daylight.

Q: What's the risk?
A: The same as always—complacency. Every other firm will rent
open-source intelligence. We'll build ours on proprietary
experience. The day we stop learning faster than our tools, we
stop deserving our clients.

The FAQ ended with a line that everyone recognized as pure
Ellis:

*We don't need more alignment. We need more curiosity.*

Outside the auditorium, the corridor became an impromptu river.
Faces he knew—older, softer; faces he didn't—bright, tired, hungry. He
shook hands until the act felt dishonest, then stopped and asked names.

"Gretchen Wolfe," she said when it was her turn. Her eyes were
the tired-but-alive look of someone who reads long into the night.

"I know the name," Bill said. "Pharma client. 'Moral imagination.'"
Her cheeks flared. "That wasn't my best day."

"It was," he said. "It just wasn't theirs."

She tried to smile and failed and then succeeded and it was better
than the first two attempts.

"You'll be there at five?" he asked.

"Wouldn't miss it," she said, and meant it with her whole face.

Two steps later: "Samir," a voice to his left. Tall, careful, gentle with his consonants.

"You built the prototype," Bill said. "The one that scared us."

"Not its fault," Samir said. "We taught it our tricks; it taught them back faster."

"You free at five?"

"I have a date with my code," Samir said. "I'll bring it."

"Bring the date," Bill said. "Shit happens when other people can see it."

He moved on. Tracy Prefontaine came to him without preamble; sharp-eyed, carrying the kind of unstudied confidence no stylist could have arranged.

"You're going to make enemies," she said.

"I came with one," Bill said. "I need counterweights."

"I'll be ballast," she said. "And keel, when needed."

"Then I'll try not to run us aground."

She nodded once. "Try harder than that."

He laughed, and it felt like stale air after riding in an elevator too long.

## ASSEMBLY

By eleven, Bill was in a smaller room with twelve associates from different offices, each chosen for one reason: someone they trusted said they told the truth even when it hurt. He wanted raw edges, not polished veneers.

He opened with no slides. "I need you to tell me what we look like from where you sit. Don't protect me. Don't flatter us. Where do we waste time? Where do we pretend?"

A woman from São Paulo spoke first. "We pretend our processes are neutral. They're not. They privilege the loud."

A man from Munich added, "We still run projects as if a perfect answer exists. Clients don't need perfection. They need momentum."

A data scientist from Bangalore said, "Our AI pilots are theater. We pick the cases that will produce pretty demos, not real decisions."

A strategist from Chicago said, "We leak condescension with tech partners. They can smell it. So can clients."

All of it pointed the same way: we're rehearsing competence while the world races ahead.

Bill wrote fast. "All right," he said, looking up. "Two things. First, we will bring clients into the kitchen. No more ta-da moments after six weeks in a black box. Second, I am chartering four Judgment Studios next week—New York, London, Singapore, Bangalore. Two real client problems each. You four will help design the first sessions. The brief is simple: show how a human and a machine, working together, reach a decision neither would alone."

The concept of the Judgment Studio was not without precedent. Decades earlier, innovation pioneers Max and Gail Taylor had created the Accelerated Solutions Environments, better known as Design Shops, to compress months of collaboration into days. Bill's Judgment Studios carried that idea into the algorithmic age, replacing paper walls with dynamic data maps but retaining the same foundation: collective intelligence, accelerated through shared purpose.

They stared at him, blinking. Then the woman from São Paulo grinned. "Finally," she said. "A lab where shouting won't help."

## A WALK AROUND THE OFFICE

After lunch, Bill walked the halls without an entourage. He stepped into cubicles unannounced, asked analysts what they were building, stopped to read whiteboards cluttered with boxes and arrows. He learned more in forty minutes than he had in forty pages the night before.

In the research library, he ran into a librarian who had been there since his first stint. She wore a scarf printed with tiny maps.

"Mr. Ellis," she said. "Back to fix us?"

"Back to listen first."

She nodded toward a stack of requests. "Do you know what's changed most? They don't ask for books anymore. They ask for prompts."

"Prompts?"

"To feed the engines," she said. "They want the fastest question to unlock the most usable answer."

Bill tapped the counter. "Tell me the best prompt you've seen in six months."

She considered it. "A head of HR asked: 'What am I not asking that will matter most in three quarters?' Our systems struggled. Eventually, a model suggested three scenarios that had nothing to do with what she'd requested in the past. Two came true."

Bill smiled. "All right," he said softly. "There's hope for us yet."

## LEADERSHIP TEAM

At three, he convened a small meeting in a conference room with windows that made the East River look closer than it was. Robert joined, as did the CFO, the CHRO, and the general counsel. He slid the First Thirty Days plan across the table.

"We're going to publish this to the whole firm by end of day," he said.

The CFO frowned. "The Contribution Ledger will trigger panic. People will call their lawyers."

"Good," Bill said. "Panic wakes the blood. And we have counsel right here."

The general counsel raised a hand. "I'll draft principles we can defend. Transparency will be key."

The CHRO leaned forward. "And the Belief Index? We'll get ugly answers."

"We need ugly answers," Bill said. "Beauty put us to sleep."

Robert studied him. "You're moving fast."

"I'm moving at the speed of attrition," Bill said. "Clients are teaching themselves how to ask better questions. We either become their favorite teacher or their last invoice."

# THE FIRST LAB MEETING

At 4:58 p.m., he pushed open the glass door to what had been a dusty war room with half-erased Gantt charts still ghosting the whiteboards. Someone had propped it open with a stack of sample decks. Someone else had dragged in a cart with a coffee urn that smelled like bark but could be forgiven for effort.

On the wall opposite the door, in blue tape and impatience, someone had spelled:

*The Lab*

Under it, a yellow Post-it note:

*Here be dragons*

A second Post-it under that:

*Good*

Twelve people. Then fifteen. Then twenty. Then enough that someone pulled chairs from the corridor and the hall and the room next door until they were sitting on the floor, on the cabinet ledges, on dignity.

Samir had brought a monitor. It showed a pulsing interface: dark, elegant, unbranded, the way a good first draft should look. Gretchen leaned in near it, half guard, half midwife.

Bill wrote four words on the whiteboard with a dry erase marker that squeaked like a tiny scream.

*Clarity. Courage. Connection. Contribution.*

He underlined each as if the line itself could dent the wall.

"These are currencies," he said. "We're broke in each of them. We're going to print our own."

He pointed to the screen. "Samir."

Samir stepped up without the nervousness of a presenter; instead, he had the nervousness of a parent introducing a child. "The model parses public and proprietary data, generates options in seconds, ranks them by the criteria we train it to respect. None of that is magic. The point is what happens after."

He clicked. The screen became a tree of possibilities, then a map of second- and third-order effects. A slider moved; ripple consequences shifted like fish in a shallow river.

"This is where we decide," Samir said. "Not what to do, but what to care about."

Gretchen took over. "And this," she said, pointing to a pane where comments stacked like a chorus, "is where someone says the thing they can't say in the partner meeting. Because the client is here, and we are all looking at the same moving picture, and it's harder to bluff when the picture is right in front of all of us."

A laugh. Relief disguised as humor.

Bill drew a small square on the board.

"Belief Index," he said. "Three questions. Monthly. The results go on that wall. Not the intranet, not an email. That wall. We'll see our faith like the way we see the weather, publicly."

A hand, hesitant. A manager from Madrid. "And if the index falls?"

"Then we stop celebrating," Bill said, "and we start asking why."

Another hand—older, hoarser. Peter Graves, the firm's unofficial archivist. "And if it rises?"

"Then we ask why harder," Bill said. "Because complacency loves a parade."

He wrote again.

*Contribution Ledger*

Under it:

*Client value (40), Innovation (30), Mentorship (20), Culture (10)*

"These weights are for this quarter," he said. "We'll argue them. Passionately. But we won't hide them."

An analyst near the door raised a hand. He was lanky, unshaven, hoodie under a blazer as if he still owed the hoodie his loyalty. "What happens when someone games it?"

"We'll design for sinners," Bill said. "And keep adjusting. That's why Gretchen is here."

Gretchen inclined her head as if accepting a sentence that fit the crime she'd asked to commit.

Two hours went like half an hour. By the end, they had a primitive sign-up sheet for Studios (a shared doc with too many simultaneous cursors), a list of clients to pilot with (three hell no and two why not?), a plan to stand up the Belief Index (anonymous, three questions, open by Monday noon, closed by Wednesday at five), and a note from an IT lead that read simply: We can make the chime.

"The chime?" Bill asked.

He'd said nothing about a chime. He'd heard it in the elevator, in the plane, in a stadium when belief was a physical pressure in the chest.

"An audible tick," the IT lead said. "When a contribution event is logged. Not loud. Not constant. Just … present."

Gretchen looked sideways at Bill. "A sound for courage," she said.

He didn't trust his voice. He nodded.

When they broke at eight, no one stood right away. The room had the quiet that follows something honest. People began washing coffee mugs, stacking chairs, wiping boards—an impulse to leave the place better than they found it.

Bill stayed to cap the markers and pick up a balled Post-it from the floor. On it, in someone's handwriting that had not learned to be careful yet:

*Maybe we're not done.*

He pocketed it like contraband.

## LANG ENCOUNTER

When the day finally let him go, the sky had turned the color of nickel, and the office had softened into evening. Bill stepped into the empty auditorium where he'd spoken that morning. The lights were low, the air cool. He took the stage again and looked out at the rows, imagining them full.

He thought of a different stage, months earlier, confetti swirling in a stadium where a band played a fight song everyone knew by muscle memory. He thought of how much work hid behind that joy: not just money or talent, but the humility to rewrite incentives, share credit, and build systems that made belief logical.

He pulled out his notebook and wrote:

> *Belief is the leading indicator.*
> *Ownership must follow contribution or none of it works.*
> *And we don't sell answers, we sell the courage to choose.*

He closed the book, slid it into his jacket, and walked toward the exit. In the doorway, he almost collided with Edward Lang.

"Evening," Lang said.

"Edward."

Lang studied him. "I won't pretend to like everything you said today."

"I won't pretend to be surprised," Bill said.

"But" Lang added, "I will say this: you made me remember a feeling I haven't had in years."

"What's that?"

Lang glanced at the stage. "The feeling that we might actually be doing something important again."

Bill held his gaze. "Help me," he said.

Lang nodded once, as if conceding a point in a long chess match. "Tomorrow," he said. "I'll bring you three sacred cows."

"Bring four," Bill said, "We'll need the practice."

## A DAY'S REFLECTION

That night, back in his office, Bill resisted the urge to open his laptop. He stood by the window instead, watching the city throw its light upward like prayers. He thought of the library prompt, 'What am I not asking that will matter most in three quarters?', and of the faces in the town hall when he'd said the word belief.

He took out his phone and typed a message to Sarah Kim:

*First day: we named the real scarce thing. Not talent. Not capital. Belief. We'll build for that.*

Her reply arrived a moment later:

*Good. Belief travels at the speed of example. Show them.*

He set the phone down, steady now. The playbook wasn't written, but the first play was. Early next week he would start the listening tour with a client who had once told Barney-Hamilton, in a moment of frustration, "You're very good at telling us what we already think." He would ask them to tell him where the firm had stopped being useful. He would stream a Judgment Studio to a skeptical Management Committee. He would invite Lang to kill one ritual he'd created himself. He would ask the librarian to join a design sprint to rewrite how the firm asked questions.

Somewhere in Ann Arbor, he imagined, the practice lights were still on, assistant coaches scripting spring installs, video analysts tagging cutups, a graduate assistant sweeping Gatorade cups from the sideline. Systems, not slogans. Belief, because the work made it rational.

Bill turned off the lamp and let the city dim to a hum.

"Welcome back," he told the darkness, and meant both the firm and himself.

He began a new entry, on a new page:

*VERITY (Introductory Description)*

*VERITY doesn't predict; it reveals. It shows us what our own decisions have been trying to say all along.*
*VERITY – Because truth requires architecture*

In his notebook, Bill sketched the outline of an idea he called VERITY. It wasn't a product yet, just a concept, half-formed and more metaphor than mechanism. VERITY, he imagined, would be a kind of mirror - part record, part diary, part conscience - pulling together the firm's scattered experience into one place.

He wrote a single line beneath the diagram:

*If we can see ourselves clearly, we might start leading ourselves honestly.*

VERITY, in that moment, was nothing more than ink on paper. But it would become the bridge between judgment and technology—the firm's most controversial, and eventually, its most transformative creation.

Outside, the city lifted its eyelids. Inside, a room remembered how to make a future.

When the building finally emptied, Bill lingered in the darkened auditorium. The only sound was the quiet hum of the AV equipment, and somewhere, faintly, the echo of his own words.

He thought about Erebus, the unseen rival that was already thinking faster than any of them could. Not malicious. Just inevitable.

He didn't fear the machine. He feared what it revealed: that the firm had stopped learning how to learn.

He opened his notebook and wrote:

> *The first revolution of intelligence ended when we forgot that wisdom doesn't scale. The next will begin when we remember that judgment does.*

Tomorrow, he'd tell Robert:

> *Before we reform the business, we reform the ownership. Until people see how their wealth depends on renewal, they'll resist it.*

He jotted one last note at the bottom of the page:

> *Incentives are the strategy. The rest is commentary.*

Then he turned off the lamp, the skyline fading into shadow, and let the thought settle into silence.

## THE NEXT MORNING

Morning brought the wet shine of a city that had not agreed to be beautiful yet was anyway. Bill walked into the office at seven. The corridor outside The Lab smelled like coffee already. On the glass wall, a printed page had been taped in basic Arial:

*Belief Index — Week One*

Blank. Waiting.

He uncapped a marker and drew a box labeled Today and two smaller boxes labeled Why and Why Not beneath it.

Gretchen appeared; the trace of a too-fast morning still on her. "You start things," she said, "and then act surprised they start."

Samir came with a laptop under his arm and a grin that broadcast sleep deprivation. "We have our first Studio volunteer," he said. "Not internal. A client."

"Who?" Bill asked.

"Novent Logistics," Samir said. "Angela wants to sit in the kitchen."

"Of course she does," Bill said, feeling it in his stomach like a new gravity. "Send her the menu. But no prices yet. We're still deciding what this costs."

"You mean what it's worth," Gretchen said.

"That too," he said.

Angela Chen had been with Novant Logistics for nearly two decades, long enough to remember when the company still called itself a freight broker and operated on instinct more than data. Bill had worked with her during his first stretch at Barney-Hamilton, guiding a turnaround that had rescued Novant from the brink. She never forgot that, or the quiet decency with which he'd done it. Over the years, their professional respect hardened into trust, though never into dependence. Angela's loyalty to Bill was real, but it was never blind; she owed him gratitude, not allegiance. Her first and only obligation was to Novant, and Bill respected her for it.

Tracy arrived with a leather folio and reading glasses perched halfway down her nose in the way of people who refuse bifocals as if they were a statement. "You're early," she told Bill, as if this were criminal.

"I didn't sleep," he said.

"Good," she said. "You'll say fewer unwise things."

At eight-fifteen, the Courage chime sounded, soft, clear. They all looked up. On VERITY, a green line ticked. Mentorship: a partner in Madrid logging an hour with two first-years. It was almost nothing. It was everything. The room went quiet in the way rooms do when someone prays.

Bill touched the whiteboard with the back of his knuckles, felt the cool through his skin, and thought, If sound can teach a building to feel, maybe a sentence can teach a firm to remember.

His phone pulsed. A message from Robert:

*Press wants a quote on "the Ellis plan.*

He typed back:

*Tell them there isn't one. There's only the firm.*

He slid the phone into his pocket, breathed once, and turned toward the day like a swimmer takes the first cold step into a lake he loves.

MARK VAN SUMEREN

CHAPTER 2

# The Listening Tour

The jet cut across a slate-gray sky, the horizon cracked open by a weak sun. Bill Ellis sat by the window, staring down at the patchwork of highways, grids, towns like constellations.

He was traveling light: one carry-on, one notebook, and the promise he'd made to the entire firm: forty client conversations in thirty days, each one a chance to hear, unvarnished, where Barney-Hamilton had stopped being useful.

He had made a similar promise years ago, when the firm still believed that listening was its sharpest instrument. Now, with AI hype rising like tidewater, he knew he had to test it again, not in headlines or investor decks, but in rooms where people whispered their doubts after the meetings ended.

Barney-Hamilton had grown large enough to forget its own pulse. VERITY was meant to reclaim it, a kind of second hearing. But as Bill watched the world tilt past the window, the same question kept nudging him:

> *If machines can answer anything, what happens to people who forget how to ask?*

## CHICAGO — THE MIRAGE OF SPEED

The plane landed under a sky of unfinished snow. Chicago in February was always halfway between defiance and fatigue. The client's tower rose from the Loop like a glass monument to efficiency.

Inside, the space gleamed: mirrored walls, posture-perfect chairs, and a screen alive with a model of their global supply chain. A vice president in a crisp suit narrated its movements as if conducting an orchestra.

"Our algorithm retrains every night," he said. "By morning, we know the market better than our competitors do."

Bill nodded, watching the blue lines ripple like veins. "And how well do you know yourselves?" he asked.

The man blinked, as though the question had come in another language.

He recovered with a laugh. "We measure everything that matters."

"That's the trick," Bill said. "Deciding what matters before you measure."

Outside, snow slid down the windows in lazy streaks. He could see the city in reflection — one skyline dissolving into another. For the first time in years, Bill wondered whether the firm's own reflection was becoming the same kind of illusion: beautiful on the surface, and hollow underneath.

He wrote in his notebook:

> *Speed feels like progress, right up until you notice you're not steering anymore.*

## ATLANTA — THE PRICE OF CERTAINTY

Atlanta greeted him with warmth and the smell of jet fuel. The air outside the terminal was thick with magnolia and motion.

The client's office was new money polished into confidence — a glass atrium, marble floors, and monitors whispering metrics in every corner. The CEO, all grin and adrenaline, clasped Bill's hand like an acquisition.

"We've cracked it," he said. "The AI engine runs our distribution. Self-optimizing, no hesitation. The beauty is it never doubts itself."

Bill smiled. "Doubt," he said softly, "is where the thinking starts."

The CEO chuckled, missing the weight of the remark. He swiped through projections on a wall display, each one perfect in its upward slope. The room glowed with certainty.

When the presentation ended, Bill lingered at the window. Planes rose and fell in the distance, steady and strangely graceful.

"My first boss used to warn me: the more perfect the information, the worse the humility."

In his notebook he wrote:

> *Confidence is not the same as competence. Algorithms confuse the two faster than people do.*

He closed the book, the sound of it sharp against the hum of the air conditioning. Outside, a thunderstorm was gathering over the horizon — slow, inevitable, righteous.

## BERLIN — THE GHOST IN THE ALGORITHM

A graphite sky hung over Berlin. Cold light pooled against the glass of the client's new headquarters — minimalist, immaculate, silent.

Inside, Bill met with Lara Weiss, the client's new strategy head. She was young and sharp, with a mind that quickened any conversation. They stood before a display of data clusters pulsing like a living organism.

"It shows me things I can't explain," she said. "Correlations I'd never imagine."

"And does it tell you which ones matter?" Bill asked.

She hesitated. "No," she admitted. "That's still my job."

He nodded. "Patterns aren't meaning. That part's still on us."

They shared a quiet moment watching the display. It looked like a constellation that didn't know its own mythology.

Before he left, she smiled and said, "Maybe we're still useful after all."

Bill replied, "You'll know you are when the machine disagrees with you and you don't flinch."

Outside, the snow had begun again, falling in a thin, soundless drift. Berlin always reminded him that progress and penance often spoke the same language.

## BANGALORE — THE COST OF TRANSLATION

Morning in Bangalore arrived in a tangle of horns and temple calls, the city already working before sunrise. Bill's car moved through the chaos like a thought trying to make sense of itself.

The firm's client here was a hospital network, proud of its predictive staffing model. The data scientists were young, brilliant, fluent in code and coffee. They showed him dashboards that shimmered, almost too pretty for what they were doing.

"It's perfect," one said. "It predicts absenteeism, demand, patient flow."

Bill nodded. "And human exhaustion?"

The room went still.

"I mean," he continued, "does it know when someone's been staring at suffering too long to see it anymore?"

They exchanged looks. One of them typed something into the model, as if the answer might be in there somewhere.

Later, on his walk back to the hotel, Bill passed a flower vendor arranging marigolds into precise rings. The petals would wilt by noon, but the care was absolute. It was devotion without profit.

He paused to buy a handful. "For no one," he said when asked who they were for. "That's the point."

In his notebook:

> *Prediction without compassion is just triage, nothing human left in it.*

# SÃO PAULO — THE WHISPER BENEATH THE METRICS

Rain washed the city into watercolor. The Barney-Hamilton office overlooked the Avenida Faria Lima, where cranes rose like punctuation marks in a sentence that never ended.

Esteves greeted him with a hug and a sigh. "You're chasing ghosts, Bill."

"I've chased worse."

They stood by the window as the rain thickened. The city was a mirror turned sideways — full of movement, short on meaning.

"Everyone wants AI," Esteves said. "No one wants to be the last to get it. But what if it makes us all the same?"

Bill smiled faintly. "Then sameness becomes the new inefficiency."

Esteves laughed. "You really think people will pay for human thinking when the machine's faster?"

"They'll pay," Bill said quietly, "when the cost of being wrong outweighs the price of being slow."

The rain softened. The city lights began to blink through like neurons in thought. For a moment, Bill imagined the entire world as one living, thinking organism, luminous and restless, unsure of itself.

# RETURN FLIGHT — THE SEED OF VERITY

The flight home left just before midnight. The cabin was half asleep, the hum of the engines a lullaby for the weary and the worried. Bill sat by the window, the world below dissolving into cloud.

He opened his notebook to a fresh page; the blank page somehow made him uneasy. He began to write:

### The Four Factors of Judgment:

*Data quality.*
*The questions we ask, and the ones we don't.*
*The values shaping how we use all of it.*
*And, finally, the expertise that decides what any of it means.*

He paused, then drew a small circle around the list. At its center, he wrote one word:

*Judgment*

He closed his eyes. The faces of the clients replayed in sequence: the pride, the awe, the quiet unease. Each of them chasing certainty through silicon.

Maybe, he thought, that was the real contagion: not technology, but the hunger for an answer that required no courage to believe.

He looked out the window. Dawn was rising over the Atlantic, the clouds below glowing like slow fire.

Somewhere in the half-light between continents, an idea began to take shape, not of a product, but of a discipline. VERITY would not be the world's next algorithmic weapon. It would be a mirror, a way to listen, to teach judgment back into intelligence.

He smiled faintly. "If wisdom can't keep up on speed," he whispered, "maybe it can win on volume."

The engines droned, steady as breath. New York was five hours ahead, waiting. And somewhere in that city, an idea was waiting to be built.

When the plane touched down, the skyline was still dark, the city holding its breath before morning. Bill stepped into the cold and felt the first stirrings of momentum.

He'd listened long enough. Now it was time to build something worth hearing.

# CHAPTER 3

# The Spark

The rain had not stopped for three days.

It came down in sheets that turned Manhattan's avenues into slick ribbons of silver and glare, the kind of rain that made the city smell faintly metallic. From his temporary office high above Bryant Park, Bill Ellis watched droplets race down the windowpane, merging and splitting, tracing small networks across the glass—joining here, breaking there, then drifting apart again. He wondered if that was how ideas behaved inside the human brain, or maybe inside Erebus.

He hadn't slept. The numbers had kept him awake: the flatline revenue and the partner withdrawals, and the quieter erosion of meaning that hid in the margins of performance reports. But it wasn't the data that haunted him; it was the feeling that something fundamental had changed while he was away, something no metric could fix.

He took a slow sip of black coffee, the kind that tasted like punishment but kept him honest and turned toward the soft knock on the glass door.

"Morning," came Samir's voice, bright but tired, half a smile buried in his beard. Gretchen Wolfe followed, carrying her tablet under one arm, rainwater darkening the shoulders of her coat. Tracy Prefontaine trailed behind them, all quiet precision and skeptical eyes. They looked like three very different answers to the same question.

Bill gestured toward the table. "Let's see it."

## THE DEMO

Samir placed his laptop on the table and connected it to the large wall display. The screen flickered, then stabilized into a dark interface that seemed to breathe. Across the top, glowing in faint gray letters:

*Erebus v3.2 — Agentic Reasoning Enabled*

"Here she is," Samir said, under his breath, like he'd just brought a live wire into the room.

The room filled with the hum of fans and the steady percussion of rain against the glass.

Gretchen crossed her arms. "We're running this from their public cloud?"

Samir nodded. "Isolated instance, air-gapped. No client data. No proprietary code. I'm not suicidal."

Bill gave a thin smile. "Good. I'd like to see what it can do before it eats us."

Samir's fingers hovered over the keyboard. "You ready?"

"Show me."

He began typing:

> *Develop a go-to-market plan for a new entrant in the European biosensor market, post-2026 regulatory alignment.*

For a heartbeat, nothing happened. Then the screen came alive—charts, tables, narrative summaries cascading into existence, one after another, as if conjured by thought itself. Within minutes, Erebus had generated a seventy-page market-entry strategy complete with competitor profiles, risk matrices, P&L projections, and recommendations for capital deployment.

The room went utterly still.

Tracy exhaled first. "That would have taken us six weeks."

"Six weeks, eight associates, and three partners," Samir added. "Give or take a few nervous breakdowns."

Bill leaned closer to the screen. The language was confident, polished—eerily familiar, as if it had stolen Barney-Hamilton's voice. He skimmed the executive summary:

> *Helios Diagnostics, market-share potential 14 percent, required investment $220 million, expected break-even at Year 3.*

He could almost hear his own consultants delivering it in well-modulated tones.

It was beautiful, just wrong.

"It sounds right," Gretchen said quietly, reading his expression. "That's the problem."

Bill turned to her. "Go on."

"It's built on public filings, scraped data, and old white papers. It's pulling noise from the world and polishing it until it sounds like sense. Look here—pricing data lifted from pre-Brexit forecasts, regulatory assumptions from a completely different sector. It's fluent," she said, "but it's basically fiction."

Tracy added, "It's got the words down. The world, not so much."

Bill nodded slowly. "So, it's us, minus the judgment."

"No," Gretchen said. "It's us, minus the scars."

## A SECOND TEST

Bill moved toward the window, watching his reflection blur against the glass. "Let's give it something real," he said. "Feed it our memory."

Samir blinked. "Our what?"

"Our Archive," Bill said. "Every engagement, every insight, every debrief we've ever stored. Anonymized, scrubbed, indexed. That's our differentiator."

Tracy frowned. "The Archive is a labyrinth. Thirty terabytes of scattered projects. It'll take days."

Bill's tone softened but carried steel. "Then start now."

Within hours, The Lab felt wired and frantic. Analysts sprinted between departments carrying encrypted drives. The hum of cooling fans rose to a steady drone. Decades of intellectual DNA—projects, case notes, interview transcripts—flowed into Samir's sandbox like blood rushing into a transplanted heart.

Bill watched from the sidelines, the way a surgeon watches the first breath after a transplant. He remembered the early days at Stone Medical, when they rebuilt the company not by cutting deeper, but by rediscovering the purpose behind the numbers. He recognized the mix, nerves and exhaustion knotted together, that had filled those rooms too.

By Friday afternoon, Samir leaned back, eyes rimmed red but alive. "Ready," he said.

"Same prompt," Bill ordered.

The screen pulsed once, then again. This time the response took longer—thirty-six seconds instead of ten. When the first paragraph appeared, Gretchen sucked in a breath.

It wasn't the same voice anymore. The language had texture. It referenced a 2011 Barney-Hamilton case on telemetry adoption, linked it to a 2019 study on patient data ethics, and cross-referenced both with a 2023 logistics simulation. The tone was careful, uncertain, human.

Tracy whispered, "It's reasoning."

Samir nodded. "It's learning from our past instead of the internet's noise."

Bill stared at the line at the bottom of the report:

> *Confidence: 89.3%. Human review recommended for ethical interpretation.*

He smiled. "It knows what it doesn't know."

"That," Tracy said, "makes it smarter than half our partners."

## THE LAB AWAKENS

They ran test after test, mergers and turnarounds, even redesigns of whole markets. Each time, Erebus-Archive produced something different: nuanced, grounded, occasionally even self-aware. It cited Barney-

Hamilton's own frameworks, weaving them into modern analysis as if the firm were arguing with its younger self.

Samir pulled up two dashboards side by side: Erebus-Public vs. Erebus-Archive.

"Noise drops from fifty-two percent to eighteen," he said. "Errors down roughly two-thirds. And the outputs are useable now."

"Translation," Gretchen said, "Our own history is the only thing that makes the machine believable."

Bill watched the screens flicker. "The open web gives you speed, Bill said. "Our memory is what gives it any shot at the truth. That's the only moat we've got."

Tracy nodded. "Curation is quality control for reality."

Bill wrote the phrase down.

## THE CLIENT TEST

Late afternoon brought a call from Robert Gaines. His face filled the video feed, pixelated and weary.

"Impressive science project," he said. "But how does it pay the rent?"

"Give me a client," Bill said.

"Novent Logistics. Angela Chen. They haven't called in a few weeks."

Minutes later, Angela appeared onscreen—sharp suit, sharper eyes, the kind of client who could smell hesitation through a monitor.

"Bill," she said. "I assume this isn't a social call."

"Not unless you've started charging for those," he said. "Give us a problem."

She smirked. "You're serious?"

"Always."

"Fine. We need to redesign our last-mile delivery network for the 2026 emissions targets. Ten minutes."

Samir began typing. The room hushed.

Nine minutes later, Erebus-Archive rendered a full network simulation—fleet optimization, emission trade-offs, policy timelines. It cited prior Barney-Hamilton work from three countries and produced a risk model accurate enough to make the CFO nervous.

Angela's jaw tightened. "You did that live?"

"Not me," Bill said. "Us. Our collective experience, distilled."

She leaned closer. "We used Erebus Labs last quarter. Their plan was fast and clean, but disastrous."

"And ours?" Bill asked.

"It's slower," she said. "But it feels real."

Bill smiled. "Speed without judgment is chaos with good manners."

For the first time, Angela Chen laughed. "Send me your proposal."

When the call ended, Gretchen whispered, "We just won back a client."

"No," Bill said. "We just won back a purpose."

## WHISPERS

Word spread overnight. By morning, half the firm was whispering about the machine that remembers.

Analysts traded screenshots like contraband. Partners hovered outside The Lab, pretending they had business nearby. Even Lang appeared, uninvited, polished and poised.

"Impressive," he said, circling the display. "You've managed to teach Erebus our tricks."

"Not tricks," Bill said. "Principles."

Lang folded his arms. "You've given it a conscience. How quaint."

Tracy glared. "You'd prefer it amoral?"

"I'd prefer it profitable," Lang said. "Erebus Labs wants a joint venture. We license them the Archive. They share revenue. Everyone wins."

Gretchen's tone was ice. "You mean we sell our soul and get a royalty check?"

Lang ignored her. "This is capitalism, not catechism."

Bill studied him for a long moment. "You sound like you've already signed."

Lang smiled faintly. "I'm just trying to keep the lights on."

Bill's voice went soft, which made it more dangerous. "If all you can imagine is survival, you've already gone dark."

## THE ARCHIVE ROOM

That night, long after everyone left, Bill wandered down to the Archive—the digital repository buried in the lower floors. The room was cool and sterile, lit by the rhythmic pulse of server lights. Each drive held fragments of the firm's past, the ghosts of decisions made and forgotten.

He walked the rows slowly, listening to the low hum of fans, shelves of drives blinking like they were thinking.

He opened a random file: Stone Medical – Vision 2020. His handwriting appeared in scanned notes: Innovation through humility.

He smiled faintly. "I believed that once."

Another file: Midwest Hospital Alliance, 1998 – Field Interviews. Voices of nurses and administrators, raw and human. He closed his eyes and could almost hear them speaking.

"This isn't data," he whispered. "It's memory."

He took out his notebook and wrote:

> *Data just piles up. Memory is what we choose to keep. Most of it is noise until someone turns it into a story. Whatever wisdom we have lives in that overlap.*

## THE NIGHT CALL

At 7 pm, his phone buzzed. Lang again.

"Bill, Erebus Labs has made a formal offer. Nine figures for the Archive IP."

Bill didn't move. "You can't sell something you don't understand."

"We own it collectively. It's partnership property."

"No," Bill said quietly. "It's our conscience. You don't sell conscience."

Lang's tone cooled. "You're a romantic, Bill. The future rewards pragmatists."

"Maybe," Bill said. "But the futures people want to live in? Romantics build those."

He hung up.

## REFLECTION

He went back upstairs to The Lab.

The servers glowed softly in the dark. Gretchen was asleep on her keyboard, a halo of blue light around her. Samir was still typing, lines of code scrolling like poetry. Tracy was on the phone, voice low, arguing with legal about data rights.

Bill stood in the doorway, watching them. They weren't consultants anymore. They were building something real out of code and all the stuff the firm usually forgot.

"These," he thought, "are the people who will teach the machine to be human."

He opened his notebook again and wrote:

> *Public data is good at prediction.*
> *Curated memory is where understanding comes from.*
> *In the end, we're defined by what we remember, and what we insist on forgetting.*

## DAWN

By morning, the rain had stopped. The city glistened, rinsed clean.

Bill stood before the whiteboard, uncapped a marker, and wrote three sentences:

> *Memory's the only real advantage that lasts.*
> *Curation looks like housekeeping, but it's leadership.*
> *AI isn't the enemy; it's the mirror.*

He underlined the last line twice. Then, as if the thought had been waiting all along, he added one more:

> *Erebus shows what's possible. VERITY must show who we are.*

He capped the marker and whispered, "Let's build our own mirror—and make sure it tells the truth."

Outside, the first commuter trains began to hum through the tunnels beneath Bryant Park. Inside, a new kind of intelligence took its first breath.

> Barney-Hamilton Internal Memorandum
> Date: January 12, 2026
> From: Office of the Managing Partner
> To: All Partners and Principals
> Subject: Introduction of VERITY
>
> VERITY: Because truth deserves architecture.
>
> Barney-Hamilton was founded on a conviction: that insight without integrity is noise.
>
> Over the years, we've built methods, models, and teams to help clients find clarity in complexity. Now we turn that discipline inward.
>
> VERITY is not a tool. It is the firm's living record of judgment, a reflection of how we think and decide, and what we've learned along the way.
>
> It connects every engagement, every dataset, every question we've ever asked, and orders them not by scale or speed, but by provenance, by the quality of the thinking that produced them.
>
> VERITY does not predict.
> It reveals.
> It listens before it answers.
> It doesn't just track what turned out to be true, it tracks what we earned the hard way.
>
> VERITY is designed to strengthen what machines cannot replicate: the human capacity for discernment.

It reminds us that intelligence, no matter how vast, remains hollow without purpose, that speed without direction is drift, and that judgment, when shared, becomes wisdom.

We built VERITY to hold ourselves accountable to the thing we claim to sell: clarity that cares about consequences.

Welcome to VERITY.

Welcome to truth, curated.

## READING THE MEMO

The email hit every inbox at 6:03 a.m., before the city's lights had fully surrendered to dawn.

In offices from London to Singapore, screens blinked awake with the same subject line:

*Introduction of VERITY: Because truth deserves architecture*

Bill Ellis read it alone in his office, coffee cooling beside an untouched stack of client reports. The snow outside muted everything — traffic, time, even thought.

He scrolled once, then stopped.

He hadn't written the words himself, not exactly — but they carried his fingerprints, softened by committee and syntax. Still, the conviction was his.

The words were simple, confident, corporate. But beneath the language, phrases like *living record of judgment*, *applied conscience*, and *clarity born of care*, he felt something older stirring.

Maybe a reckoning. Maybe a promise. Hard to tell which yet.

Down the hall, he could hear Gretchen's voice, brisk and measured, already discussing integration timelines. Samir was probably in The Lab, running new simulations before sunrise. The firm was moving again — faster, louder, certain.

Bill leaned back, reread the final line.

*Welcome to truth, curated.*

He smiled — not with pride, but with recognition.

They had built a mirror, whether they knew it or not. And soon, it would start to look back.

VERITY's code sat atop of The Archive — decades of reports, transcripts, and client histories that once defined the firm's intellect. The Archive remembered what Barney-Hamilton had done; VERITY was built to understand why. One stored knowledge. The other searched for meaning. Together, they were the firm's memory, finally learning how to think.

He closed the message and turned toward the glass wall.

Outside, the city shimmered faintly in reflection, bright and restless, unaware that something inside Barney-Hamilton had just come alive.

CHAPTER 4

# VERITY

Snow had long since melted from the skyline, but inside Barney-Hamilton's midtown tower, winter still clung to the air, crisp and bright, with an edge of something waiting to thaw.

Bill Ellis stood at the glass wall of The Lab, looking out over the gray shimmer of morning. Down below, the city seethed in its usual impatience: taxis leaning on horns, pedestrians weaving, steam venting from manholes like the city's own breath. Up here, silence ruled, save for the low hum of servers waking from sleep.

The day after the Erebus demonstration felt like the morning after a cancer diagnosis: still standing, but never the same.

He sipped his coffee, lukewarm, bitter—and smiled at the absurdity that he could rescue billion-dollar companies yet could never remember to drink while it was hot.

Across the room, Gretchen Wolfe was already at work, half-hidden behind a constellation of screens, her focus so taut it felt one insight away from mutiny.

"Morning," he said.

She didn't look up. "You should see this."

She flicked her wrist, and the main display woke, revealing a diagram labeled VERITY.

Bill stepped closer.

Three circles overlapped: Memory, Expertise, Belief, forming a faintly glowing Venn diagram on the screen.

"This isn't your Belief Index anymore," he said.

"No," she replied. "It's everything."

## THE PROTOTYPE

Samir arrived next, late only by his own impossible standards, laptop dangling from one hand, a protein bar from the other. "Don't panic," he said, "but I think we've built something alive."

He connected the laptop to the wall display. Instantly, the screen filled with nodes and filaments, each pulsing softly, the way a heartbeat looks on a monitor.

"Each node is a project," Samir explained, "drawn from the Archive. The lines between them are shared insights and methods, sometimes even people. The machine is mapping how Barney-Hamilton thinks."

Bill stared. It looked like a neuron firing.

He thought of the first time he'd seen an angiogram at Stone Medical—those pulsing rivers of blood revealing the body's secret highways. This was the same, just wired for thought instead of blood.

"Watch what happens when you click a node," Samir said.

He tapped one labeled Rural Care Delivery 2023. Instantly, two dozen more lit up:

*Telemedicine Reimbursement 2015, Insurance Equity Model
2019, Patient Access Index 2021*

"VERITY recognizes patterns we never recorded," Samir said. "It's learning our instincts."

What emerged over time, was not just a tool but a framework for disciplined intelligence. They eventually gave its logic four pillars:

> *Memory* – the curated data.
> *Inquiry* – the way they sharpened the questions.
> *Ethics* – the values that put guardrails on its use.
> *Judgment* – the expertise that decided what if any of it meant.

Together they made something more than a tool; they found a way to keep speed from overrunning integrity.

Bill felt a small shiver. "We're building a second brain."

Gretchen smiled. "No, Bill. We're mapping our first one. We just never knew what it looked like."

## THE VISION MEETING

By mid-morning, the core team gathered. Tracy Prefontaine leaned against the window, arms crossed, skeptical by default. Robert Gaines joined via video, his tie slightly askew, his face pale in New York's winter light.

Bill stood before the screen.

"VERITY started as a way to measure belief," he said. "Now it's the foundation for how we think. Erebus showed us what happens when intelligence moves faster than judgment: it creates confident nonsense. VERITY is meant to do the opposite, to slow our thinking just enough to make it mean something."

He pointed to the three glowing circles.

> *Memory. Our curated Archive—sixty-eight years of experience, scrubbed and indexed. Not nostalgia. Navigation.*

> *Expertise. A living map of who knows what, and how. It breaks hierarchy. It replaces titles with capability.*

> *Belief. The cultural signal—the rhythm that tells us whether we're growing or rotting.*

Tracy raised an eyebrow. "And you want to make all this visible?"

"Yes. Radical transparency. Shine enough light on the truth, and politics has nowhere to hide."

Robert's voice crackled. "You'll have partners terrified to see themselves in that mirror."

"Then we'll start with courage," Bill said.

## RESISTANCE

Halfway through the meeting, the door opened and Edward Lang entered. Crisp and precise, every line of him was sharpened by skepticism.

"I hear we're crowdsourcing our conscience," he said dryly.

"Something like that," Bill replied.

Lang paced slowly around the table, studying the projections. "And what happens when VERITY tells us our heroes have been wrong? When our best clients hate what they see?"

"Then we listen," Bill said.

Lang turned, eyes narrowing. "You're proposing to make every mistake and hesitation, even our flaws, transparent. That's not leadership. That's self-immolation."

Bill met his gaze. "Transparency isn't suicide, Edward. It's sunlight. The only people who fear it are those who've forgotten how to grow."

He didn't answer. Lang was a man who trusted control more than people.

For a moment, Lang heard his own words echo back at him and wondered when he had started mistaking caution for wisdom. VERITY terrified him not because it was wrong, but because it no longer needed men like him to interpret the fog. He'd built a career on being the bridge between power and uncertainty. Now, he saw a system that looked like it could cross the river without him.

## JUDGMENT STUDIO

The Studios represented an evolution of the Design Shop model that had once transformed organizational problem-solving. Where the Taylors' environments relied on visualization and facilitation, these new rooms added an AI layer, machines capable of surfacing connections and contradictions, and mapping out the consequences in real time. The essence, however, was unchanged: a structured space where judgment could be seen, tested, and strengthened.

That afternoon, the first official Judgment Studio convened.

A cross-disciplinary team faced a live client challenge: a global energy consortium reeling from volatile carbon-credit markets.

Erebus and VERITY were linked for the first time. The interface shimmered as the system pulled threads from old engagements, merging public data with Barney-Hamilton's proprietary experience.

Within minutes, it had generated a scenario map so detailed it looked like a living atlas: policy forecasts and market pressures, laid out alongside ethical trade-offs.

Tracy raised a hand. "Pause it."

The simulation froze mid-motion.

"There," she said, pointing. "That assumption—it's statistically correct but ethically blind. Erebus can't see the moral weight."

Gretchen added, "It doesn't know what 'should' feels like."

Bill nodded. "That's where we come in. Machines can compute all they want. We decide what deserves to exist."

The client team watched, transfixed.

"This," Bill said quietly, "isn't consultancy. It's co-creation."

## BELIEF HAS A BALANCE SHEET

Weeks passed.

VERITY absorbed terabytes of data, building neural pathways through decades of projects. It began surfacing correlations no one had considered, linking employee engagement with client renewal and innovation metrics with cultural health.

Late one night, Gretchen found Bill alone, staring at a new dashboard.

"What am I looking at?" she asked.

He pointed.

*Belief Index vs. Client Retention. High-belief teams outperform low-belief ones by twenty-two percent.*

She blinked. "You're saying morale drives profit?"

"I'm saying faith does," Bill said softly. "Belief is a leading indicator."

He scribbled in his notebook:

*If faith had a balance sheet, trust would be the capital line and transparency the way you did the books.*

He closed the notebook, feeling something shift inside him—an echo of the moment Michigan football had rediscovered its soul, rewriting its playbook without selling its integrity. VERITY was his version of NIL, an act of modernity born from memory.

## THE MANAGEMENT COMMITTEE

Two weeks later, the boardroom filled with partners and committee members. VERITY glowed behind Bill like a living galaxy.

"Erebus proved intelligence is abundant," he said. "VERITY proves wisdom is rare. It's not a dashboard. It's an operating system. A place where AI, data, and belief converge."

He showed them the new interface: client projects mapped by insight density; belief trends charted against innovation velocity.

"Our moat," he said, "is not secrecy. It's curation. Every other firm will feed their agents public noise. We'll feed ours sixty-eight years of earned knowledge and the moral context that shaped it."

Lang sat forward. "And you think that's defensible?"

"Yes," Bill said. "Because no algorithm can convincingly fake a conscience. Not for long."

The room fell silent.

Then Robert Gaines spoke quietly. "Then let's build it."

## MIDNIGHT AT THE LAB

The office emptied. Only the hum of machines remained. Bill stood by the glass, city lights reflected in VERITY's screen.

A notification pulsed in the corner:

*New Belief Entry: 'Hope'.*

He smiled and wrote on the whiteboard:

*If Erebus is the brain, VERITY is the soul.*

Then, almost as an afterthought, he added beneath it:

*Belief is the oxygen intelligence runs on.*

The words glowed faintly under the overhead light.

He turned off the room's lamps, leaving only VERITY's soft pulse to illuminate the dark, like the heart of something new, beating in the body of something old.

## NOTEBOOK – REFLECTIONS

*Memory is our accumulated truth.*
*Expertise is the muscle that wields it.*
*Belief is the blood that keeps it alive.*

*VERITY is where all three meet.*
*It is not a system; it's a mirror that remembers.*

*Every generation drops some of what it once believed.*
*Maybe VERITY lets us remember faster than we forget.*

*Leadership isn't about calling tomorrow. It's about getting today to remember soon enough to change.*

## CLOSING SCENE

Dawn slid across the skyline, pale and cold. Bill stepped into the empty corridor, the sound of his shoes soft against the marble. He looked through the glass one last time at the glow of The Lab.

He thought of Michigan again—of the banner, the roar, the words, *Those Who Stay Will Be Champions.*

He whispered, almost to himself, "Those who remember will be leaders."

Then he walked into the light of morning, ready to build a future worth remembering.

# CHAPTER 5

# Listening Tour Redux

The winter train slid out of Penn Station under a hard, steel-gray sky. Snow threatened but never committed, smearing the city into a kind of holding-pattern gray. Bill Ellis sat by the window, coat collar turned up, a notebook balanced on one knee. Beside him, a cup of coffee had cooled into resignation.

Outside, New Jersey blurred by in a collage of warehouses, switchyards, and half-frozen rivers. Inside, the rhythm of the rails matched the one thought he couldn't silence: The firm was forgetting how to listen.

VERITY had done everything the press releases promised: it dazzled and scaled, and it impressed the right people. Clients quoted its insights; investors called it "a moat in motion." But Bill had seen the other side of brilliance. Beneath the noise of metrics and applause, Barney-Hamilton was drifting, not failing, yet, but losing the quiet humility that once made its intelligence human.

He tapped his pen against the notebook and wrote one line:

*Machines can answer anything now. What happens if we forget how to ask?*

Then he closed the book, leaned back, and watched the gray fields roll past.

## DETROIT – THE FIRST FACTOR: THE QUALITY OF DATA

The client's Detroit office sat in a repurposed auto-parts warehouse: high ceilings and glass walls above concrete floors still scuffed by the old machine lines. Someone had left a mural from the old factory days untouched:

*Hands Build Futures*

The irony wasn't lost on him.

He met Denise Morales, a COO who carried the unshakable calm of someone who had survived both bankruptcy and rebirth. She led him through a floor of engineers now fluent in algorithms instead of torque.

"You people saved us," she said, gesturing toward a production dashboard glowing cobalt blue. "But not because you gave us a model. You listened. You helped us see what was in front of us."

Bill smiled.

"The data was already there," he said. "You just needed someone to help it make sense."

That was the first factor of judgment: the quality of the data curated. Not quantity. Not velocity. Quality. The useful stuff is earned, not scraped. Machines could collect everything; wisdom meant deciding what not to keep.

As he left the office, the snow began to fall — thin, uncertain. Detroit, he thought, understood reinvention because it had buried itself before. The sound of the wind against the old steel panels sounded half like a lament, half like a promise.

## DALLAS – THE SECOND FACTOR: THE PRECISION OF QUESTIONS

In Dallas, heat shimmered off the tarmac, even in February. The office smelled of coffee and whiteboard ink, and of people trying a little too hard to sound sure of themselves. The firm's regional partner, Chan Wu, met him in a conference room lit by afternoon glare. She had the clipped intensity of someone who had grown allergic to pretense.

"We keep asking it the same things," she said, pointing at VERITY display. "It keeps giving us the same answers."

Bill chuckled softly. "Then it's learning from us too well."

He leaned over her screen. The questions were all framed for efficiency: "What's optimal?" "What's the market signal?" and, inevitably, "What's the margin sensitivity?" None of them asked why the signal mattered, or to whom.

That was the second factor: the precision of the questions posed.

The machine was only as wise as the curiosity that trained it. Inquiry without any imagination is just another kind of automation.

He wrote in his notebook:

> *Good judgment usually doesn't start with better data. It starts with questions that are a little braver.*

When he looked up, Chan was watching him. "You sound like a professor."

He smiled. "Professors get tenure. I get turbulence."

## SÃO PAULO – THE THIRD FACTOR: HUMAN VALUES

Rain fell sideways in São Paulo, turning Avenida Faria Lima into a ribbon of reflections. The local office pulsed with youth, analysts in sneakers, and dashboards on glass walls, with laughter that didn't wait for permission.

Bill walked the rows, pausing at a display where VERITY visualized client sentiment in waves of color. Red marked risk, green showed alignment, and gold meant conviction. The room glowed like a chapel made of dashboards.

Esteves, the regional lead, approached. "Clients love the speed," he said. "But some are asking — does it still feel like us? Does it know what we stand for?"

Bill turned, the rain blurring the skyline behind him. "That's the right question."

The third factor of judgment was the human values that governed its application.

Without some conscience behind it, intelligence turns into just another weapon. AI didn't invent bias; it just automated the ones people refused to see.

He wrote later that night, in the hotel bar lit by a single flickering bulb:

> *Technology amplifies everything, including the character of the people using it.*

He closed his notebook and ordered another coffee. The storm outside raged without apology.

## SINGAPORE – THE FOURTH FACTOR: EXPERTISE IN INTERPRETATION

The Singapore office sat above Marina Bay, glass on water, reflection on reflection. In the morning light, the city looked engineered for optimism.

A young strategist named Aisha led Bill through The Lab's newest deployment. On a wall-sized display, VERITY mapped outcomes with the elegance of origami. Models nested inside models, each scenario pulsing like the heartbeat of possibility.

"It's brilliant," she said. "But it doesn't tell you which future to choose."

Bill smiled. At last.

The fourth factor was the professional expertise brought to bear when interpreting output.

Data can describe the world. Experience decides what to do about it.

He told her, "That's why we'll never be replaced. Machines can simulate intellect, but not consequence."

She tilted her head. "So, judgment is our last proprietary asset?"

"Exactly," he said. "And, weirdly, it's the only one that grows when we share it around."

They stood there a while longer, watching the model unfold like a thought made visible.

## THE SYNTHESIS – THE FOUR FACTORS OF JUDGMENT

Back in New York, Bill's office was dark except for the glow of the skyline. He sat at his desk and drew a square in his notebook. At each corner he wrote one word:

*Data*                    *Questions*

*Values*                  *Expertise*

In the center, he wrote:

*Judgment*

He underlined it twice.

The firm had once worshiped Strategy, Operations, Finance, and Transformation — tidy boxes for tidy minds. But that language belonged to an age of process, not discernment.

These new Four Factors weren't departments; they were disciplines — a way to keep any kind of wisdom alive in a world obsessed with speed.

*Curated data gave us something solid to stand on.*
*Better questions gave us direction.*
*Values kept it from drifting into something ugly.*
*And expertise was what turned it all into decisions that meant something.*

Take any one away and you don't get intelligence; you get automation: fast and sure of itself, but hollow.

He looked out the window. The city pulsed with a billion lights, each a fragment of someone's certainty. "The world doesn't need faster minds," he murmured. "It needs steadier hands."

## THE WINDOW

A week later, Gretchen appeared at his door, arms crossed, eyes tired but kind.

"You're really doing it," she said. "Listening."

"Trying to."

"So, what did you hear?"

He turned toward the window. "That we've spent months asking who should own us. But the better question is: what do we own that no one else can?"

She waited. "And what's that?"

"Judgment," he said. "Refined by time and shared on purpose. And most importantly of all, held up by belief."

She smiled faintly. "Sounds expensive."

"It is," he said, still watching the city's lights shimmer like data points on an infinite grid. "That's why we can't sell it."

He opened his notebook one last time and wrote:

*If intelligence is everywhere now, wisdom must be deliberate.*

Then he closed the cover. The night reflected his face back at him, older and steadier, but finally certain of one thing: listening was the beginning of leadership.

## REFLECTIONS ON OWNERSHIP AND CHANGE

(Bill's Notebook — March 3)

The partners were arguing about price; Bill was thinking about patience.

It struck him that the more sophisticated the firm became, the more primitive its instincts turned. VERITY had made them visible, measurable, and desirable again. Investors saw leverage; analysts saw optionality. But Bill saw noise — the kind that precedes confusion.

He wrote at the top of the page:

*Form follows function*

The phrase had anchored him since the tours. Every factory, office, and boardroom had shown him the same truth: enduring systems reveal their structure only after their purpose is clear. A bridge isn't defined by its owners; it's defined by what it must span.

So too with Barney-Hamilton.

Private equity, he knew, was not the enemy. It was a tool, powerful and impatient, and, if mishandled, corrosive. The right investor could amplify the firm's reach; the wrong one could dissolve its coherence overnight. What frightened him wasn't the capital, but the conditionality that always followed it: new governance, new incentives, new definitions of value.

He wrote:

> *Sell too early and whatever moat you had starts to leak.*
> *License too soon and the IP decays into just another commodity.*

The firm's value, he reminded himself, didn't live in code or contracts. It lived in its judgment architecture, the integration of its Four Factors: Curated Data, Precise Questions, Human Value, and Expert Synthesis. Each was proprietary not because it was secret, but because it was earned. Sixty-eight years of client scars and recoveries, crises and recoveries again: the iterative craft of deciding wisely under uncertainty.

He paused, considering VERITY. Its brilliance was undeniable, but it was only the latest instrument in a much older orchestra. What gave VERITY its intelligence was not its algorithms but the way Barney-Hamilton's people framed the question and exerted its wisdom when determining what to do with its output. It wasn't a machine of answers; it was a mirror for judgment.

Licensing that too early, Bill thought, would be like publishing a language before teaching anyone to speak it.

He turned the page and drew the familiar square again.

At each corner he wrote the Factors:

> *Curated Data*     *Precise Questions*
>
> *Human Value*     *Expert Synthesis*

In the center:

> *Moat*

Beneath it:

*Belief*

He added one more word in the margin —

*Equity*

If belief was to endure, ownership had to follow it. Not to Wall Street, but to the people who gave the firm its mind and conscience. Partners, associates, analysts — they carried the intellectual capital that made VERITY meaningful. Without meaningful equity, they would become contractors to their own creation.

He closed the notebook and sat back. The city was dark beyond his window, its rhythm pulsing like a metronome of decisions yet to be made.

The ownership question wasn't about price. It was about protection: of how the firm worked, how it thought, and why anyone believed in it.

Form would follow soon enough.

## REFLECTIONS ON OWNERSHIP AND CHANGE (CONTINUED)

(Bill's Notebook — March 7)

He began a new entry, on a new page.

*The Architecture of Ownership and Change*

*Ownership isn't a category. It's just a way of designing for patience.*

He drew three columns across the page —

*Private Equity     Partnership        Public Company*

and began to think through each.

*Private Equity: Capital With Character*

He started with the most misunderstood model of all.

*Private equity isn't automatically bad. It's just impatient capital looking for a grown-up in the room.*

He had seen both kinds: the ruthless operators who carved value out of payrolls and the long-horizon investors who cultivated it through stewardship. The difference wasn't structure; it was intent.

> *The great PE firms don't buy broken companies to flip them. They find sound companies with solid fundamentals and exceptional leadership that simply lack the capital to grow. They don't dictate strategy—they oxygenate it.*

He remembered one, a family-backed fund that helped Stone Medical finance its new manufacturing facility when no bank would take the risk. "They didn't lecture us about EBITDA," he wrote. "They asked what we could build if someone finally believed."

That was the kind of investor he respected—the one who treated capital not as a cudgel but as a covenant.

> *The problem isn't private equity; it's how short the half-life of its ambition can be. The best funds plant oaks; the worst plant annuals. Long-horizon funds build cathedrals. The short-cycle ones just throw up scaffolding. You can tell which you have by whether the playbook starts with growth or cost-cutting.*

He paused, remembering a conversation years ago with Tommy Frist at HCA. Bill could still hear Frist's soft Tennessee drawl: "We had to shrink to grow, Bill. Easier to do when you don't have to explain yourself to Wall Street every ninety days." When HCA went private in 2006, it was to shed the weight of visibility—to divest quietly, reorganize brutally, and emerge renewed. The strategy had worked. Sometimes the only way to save an institution was to hide it long enough to heal.

> *HCA did it right. They stepped away from the public glare to right-size and retool, not to strip assets, but to restore discipline. They came back stronger. That's what short-term pain in service of long-term purpose looks like.*

He underlined the phrase short-term pain, long-term purpose.

### *The Partnership: Stewardship Or Stagnation?*

Next, he turned to the model closest to home—the partnership.

> *Partnerships begin with noble intent: shared ownership and responsibility, and a kind of shared pride. But over time, they calcify. They become federations of self-interest disguised as stewardship.*

The partnership model rewarded what partners could distribute, not what they could build. In-year earnings were sacred. Investment was seen as subtraction. Transformation—anything with a multi-year payoff—required near-revolutionary courage.

> *It's hard to ask a partner to think like an owner when their paycheck depends on being a renter of the present.*

He had watched it countless times: brilliant partners sabotaging long-term projects because the return wouldn't hit this fiscal year.

> *A partnership without reinvestment is a pension plan in disguise.*

### *The Public Company: Transparency And Tyranny*

He shifted to the public markets, the temple of accountability and anxiety.

> *Public companies breathe in quarters and exhale press releases. The market rewards predictability, but transformation triggers volatility.*

He had watched CEOs try to reconcile the two—one hand steadying the ship for analysts, the other trying to steer toward change.

> *Boards say they want boldness but punish deviation. Analysts want growth, but not the turbulence it requires.*

And yet, public companies had virtues: discipline, transparency, liquidity.

*The best ones run two calendars—one for investors, one for innovators. The first measures precision; the second measures progress.*

### The Nonprofit: The Virtue and the Quagmire

Then, Bill turned to a model too often romanticized—the nonprofit.

He had worked with hospitals, universities, and more than a few charities. All noble, all well-intentioned, all chronically slow.

*Nonprofits live in a democracy of noble intentions. Their capital is moral, not financial. Their shareholders are physicians, donors, trustees, and public opinion—and none of them ever agree at the same time.*

He thought back to his consulting years with health systems. Meetings that began with passion and ended in paralysis. He could still hear the refrain: 'We need more input before we decide.'

*Consensus is noble but it's slow. In for-profits, capital speeds the clock. In nonprofits, virtue dilutes it. Decisions migrate to committees designed to protect everyone's point of view, and as a result, no one's urgency.*

He smiled ruefully and scribbled these lines:

*No one ever lost their job for scheduling another committee meeting.*

*The irony is that freedom from shareholder pressure should make nonprofits the most innovative. Instead, it often makes them the most cautious. The absence of a financial imperative creates an overabundance of procedural ones.*

Still, he didn't judge them harshly.

*Mission has a gravity all its own. It keeps people honest—even when it keeps them slow.*

### The Unifying Rule

He drew a heavy line beneath the page and summarized what experience had already taught him.

> *Every ownership model builds wealth differently and that determines how it tolerates change.*
> *Private equity builds wealth by multiplying capital. So, it demands acceleration.*
> *Public companies build wealth by sustaining valuation. So, they demand predictability.*
> *Partnerships build wealth by distributing profit. So, they demand continuity.*
> *Nonprofits build wealth by preserving virtue. So, they demand consensus.*
> *Each one is allergic to change in its own way.*
> *Private equity flinches at uncertainty.*
> *Public markets flinch at real disruption.*
> *Partnerships flinch at reinvention.*
> *Nonprofits flinch at conflict.*

He wrote one final line, in darker ink:

> *If you want to change a system, first follow the money—and then ask how patient it really is.*

He underlined "patient" twice.

Then, almost as an afterthought, he added a postscript at the bottom of the page:

> *The ownership model doesn't determine wisdom—only how fast wisdom has to show up.*

He stared at it for a long moment, closed the notebook, and whispered, "Before we reform the business, we reform the clock."

He had been writing more than he was sleeping. The nights came and went in fragments, half-thoughts, sketches of frameworks, sentences that began as strategy and ended as confession.

On the seventh page, he wrote a heading and underlined it twice:

*Function Before Form*

The Listening Tours had taught him that the firm's advantage wasn't mystical or accidental. It was earned, codified through time, and sharpened through repetition. The Four Factors were not just abstractions; they were habits of excellence. They gave Barney-Hamilton a language for judgment that no algorithm could replicate.

But those habits were under siege. VERITY's success had drawn attention the firm was not ready to bear. Clients saw certainty. Investors saw scalability. Partners saw liquidity. Everyone saw something different, and in the noise, the discipline of the Four Factors was fading.

Bill drew a line down the center of the page and began listing what he knew.

Left column:

*Strengths:*

> *Proprietary Judgment Architecture*
> *Collective Intellectual Capital*
> *Cultural Trust and Candor*

Right column:

*Risks:*

> *Fragmented Ownership Incentives*
> *Shallow Understanding of VERITY's Moat*
> *External Pressure to Monetize Prematurely*

He circled the last line twice. That, he realized, was the new fault line — the one that could split the firm from itself.

He wrote beneath it:

*We cannot sell what we have not yet defined.*

Then, slowly, he began outlining what would come next.

First, the partners needed to see what he had seen — not just the technology, but the architecture of judgment it amplified. They needed to revisit the Four Factors, to ground themselves again in the firm's intellectual core.

Second, they needed to surface the tension between ownership and purpose. Equity had to migrate toward contribution — to the people who refined the moat daily, not those who merely managed it. If belief was to scale, it needed ownership to follow its contours.

Finally, they needed to quiet the noise. No more speculation about offers or licensing deals until the function was clear.

He paused, thinking of Edward Lang. Of the precision that had curdled into resistance. Of how easily intellect turned defensive when its relevance felt threatened.

Bill underlined a line he'd written earlier in the margins of another page:

*Authority doesn't protect relevance. Curiosity does.*

He felt a clarity he hadn't in months. The decision to sell or license was no longer the question. The question was what must endure — and what ownership structure would serve that endurance, not the other way around.

He closed the notebook, pressing his palm against the cover until the leather warmed. In the silence, the city's hum returned — taxis, air vents, the faint murmur of motion that always reminded him of persistence.

For the first time in weeks, he felt aligned with the rhythm.

He whispered the words he would use to open an upcoming partner meeting:

*Before we decide who owns Barney-Hamilton, we must decide what Barney-Hamilton owns.*

# CHAPTER 6

# The Tipping Point

VERITY came alive on a Wednesday.

Not all at once, but like a sunrise, edges first, faint and curious at the start, then spilling into every corner of the firm. Overnight, servers spun to life in London, Singapore, São Paulo, and Chicago. Analysts logged in expecting another dashboard and instead found something alive, breathing light and questions.

It asked them things.

*What did you learn this week?*
*Who taught you?*
*What surprised you?*

No forms. No compliance boxes. Just questions, waiting instead of lecturing.

By mid-morning, VERITY had three thousand active users. By nightfall, twelve thousand. Within a week, Barney-Hamilton's chatter had changed. People no longer spoke of decks or deliverables; they spoke of contributions.

The word had weight again.

## THE LAB

Bill Ellis watched from the glass wall of The Lab as data rendered itself into motion. VERITY's neural map now stretched across six continents, glowing like a city grid viewed from orbit.

Samir sat hunched over two monitors, eyes red-rimmed, the way engineers look when they've crossed from fatigue into awe. Gretchen was on her third coffee, posture taut, orchestrating comments from field offices with the precision of someone holding the whole firm together by will. Tracy stood near the whiteboard, her skepticism replaced by something resembling faith.

"This is what scale looks like," Samir said quietly. "Belief, running at bandwidth."

Bill didn't respond. He was watching a node in Singapore pulse, connect to another in São Paulo, then split into three more, questions leaping oceans faster than the firm's planes ever could.

He felt both exhilaration and dread. Scale was a gift that came wrapped in risk.

## LONDON

Across the Atlantic, the London office hummed under rain and unease. VERITY had exposed what years of PowerPoint never had, patterns of neglect, silos of expertise hoarded like currency.

At 10:07 a.m., a quiet explosion occurred in the firm's internal forum. A partner in Infrastructure posted anonymously:

*If belief is currency, some of us have been printing counterfeit.*

Within an hour, it had hundreds of responses. Some defensive, others brutally honest.

Elena Martínez, head of London operations, called Bill directly.

"Your little experiment," she said, "has started a revolution in HR."

Bill leaned back in his chair, rubbing his eyes. "Good. Revolutions cost less than another round of layoffs."

"Until they don't," she replied.

## THE LEAK

By Friday, word reached him from Singapore: Erebus Labs had launched a new campaign: 'Memory Without Borders.'

Their marketing was unmistakable.

Tagline:

*Why buy expertise when you can rent it?*

The visuals mimicked Barney-Hamilton's VERITY branding, down to the concentric circles.

Samir slammed his laptop shut. "They've cloned us."

Gretchen shook her head. "No. They've plagiarized us badly. But they're faster."

Bill felt the old familiar pressure in his chest—the one he'd had at Stone Medical before Vision 2020. It wasn't fear; it was a spark.

He called Robert.

"They're using our language."

"Everyone uses everyone's language, Bill."

"Not when it means something."

## INTERNAL WEATHER

The following Monday, VERITY's Belief Index flickered red in two offices: Dubai and Chicago. Anonymous comments flooded the feed.

*VERITY watches but doesn't protect.*
*We're afraid transparency is a prelude to punishment.*
*Belief without boundaries is surveillance.*

Tracy found Bill staring at the wall display late that night, the red nodes pulsing like open wounds.

"They're not wrong," she said. "We've built omniscience without consent."

Bill exhaled. "The line between accountability and exposure is thin."

"Then draw it," she said. "Before someone else does."

## THE BREACH

The next morning, a confidential notice hit his inbox:

*SUBJECT: Data Integrity Alert: London Node Compromised*

One of the partners, a rising star named Marcus Levy, had exported client fragments from VERITY to a private server—then offered access to Erebus Labs under a nondisclosure agreement.

Robert called within minutes. "Do you know about this?"

"I do now."

"Legal wants to suspend him quietly. No press."

"No," Bill said. "We do it publicly. The firm needs to see consequence."

"Bill, that's suicide."

"It's surgery."

Within an hour, a firm-wide message went out under Bill's signature:

*Integrity Announcement: VERITY is built on trust. Breaching it forfeits membership in this community. Effective immediately, Marcus Levy's partnership is terminated.*

Transparency begins at home.

It was the most-read internal message in the firm's history.

By evening, VERITY's Belief Index turned green again.

## CONFRONTATION

Edward Lang arrived unannounced at Bill's office that night, the door closing behind him with courtroom precision.

"Public execution," he said. "You've just set a precedent no one can live with."

"I've set one no one should live without."

Lang paced, his movements measured and controlled. "You think fear will teach ethics? You're wrong. It breeds resentment."

Bill looked up. "You're confusing fear with respect."

Lang stopped. "You're confusing respect with obedience."

Lang wanted to believe he was defending principle, not position. But somewhere between the words, he felt the tremor of irrelevance—the sense that the place was starting to speak a language he didn't quite follow anymore. He covered it, as always, with precision.

Silence stretched between them.

Finally, Bill said, "You still treat leadership like it's about control. It isn't. It's about giving people enough context to decide. VERITY gives us that. For the first time in decades, people can see cause and effect in real time—belief translating into outcomes, contribution into equity. That's not control; that's clarity."

Lang's jaw tightened. "And clarity is what kills mystique. Without mystique, we're just another services firm with better fonts."

Bill smiled thinly. "Then let mystique go. I'd rather be boring and honest than legendary and hollow."

Lang stared at him a moment longer, then turned to leave. "Careful, Bill. You're turning transparency into religion."

"Maybe," Bill said. "But at least it has commandments."

## THE CLIENT REVOLT

Two weeks later, the headlines broke.

*Erebus Outperforms Barney-Hamilton in Global Pharma Simulation*

The article wasn't wrong. A top pharmaceutical client, Athara Biogen, had quietly used Erebus to model a new market-entry plan. They publicly credited it for shaving six months off their product launch, compared to a plan previously developed by Barney-Hamilton.

Bill saw the news first in his morning feed. By the time he reached the office, the firm's internal chat was on fire. Partners questioned whether their analog conscience could keep pace with a synthetic rival that didn't sleep or moralize.

At noon, his assistant appeared in the doorway. "Athara's CEO on line one."

He picked up. "Barbara."

"It's not me this time," she said. "It's the market. Erebus just proved speed wins. You can't fight that."

"I don't want to fight it," Bill said. "I want to finish it."

She paused. "You sound like you have a plan."

"Invite me to your next board meeting," he said. "I'll show you what Erebus missed."

## THE BOARDROOM DUEL

Athara's global headquarters sat like a glass citadel above the Hudson, all angles and arrogance.

Bill arrived with Gretchen and Samir. The room was lined with directors in dark suits, each wearing the polite skepticism reserved for consultants past their prime.

Barbara Green opened. "Erebus delivered a plan in four hours. Convince us why we should pay humans for the same."

Bill nodded. "May I see its plan?"

She handed him a tablet. He skimmed, frowning. "Elegant. But empty."

"How so?"

"It assumes regulators behave like math. They don't. It assumes patients adopt technology like markets. They don't. It assumes your competitors stand still. They never do. Erebus sees patterns; it doesn't see people."

Samir projected a map from VERITY—Athara's historic launches, clinician feedback, cultural barriers, public trust metrics—drawn not from the internet but from sixty-eight years of experience.

"Erebus missed the soft data," Gretchen said. "The kind that doesn't fit a spreadsheet but decides whether a product lives or dies."

Take your launch curve," Bill said. "Erebus assumes physicians switch because the data tells them to. But we've interviewed hundreds of them over the years. They switch because they trust the story behind the data. And your story," he added gently, "is still recovering from a safety scare that never made headlines but changed the mood in three major markets. Erebus can't feel that. We can."

"And here," Bill continued, gesturing to the financial model, "Erebus prices the therapy as if payers are spectators. They aren't. We've already seen two of them preparing hurdles that don't appear in public filings. Erebus can't catch what isn't published. VERITY can, because it remembers everything, we've learned with you, not just what's online."

Bill turned to the board. "Erebus gives you intelligence. VERITY gives you judgment. You can license speed. You can't license sense, not the kind you need."

The room went still. Angela leaned back, smiling faintly. "Send me a proposal."

Outside the boardroom, Gretchen whispered, "We just stole back the future."

Bill shook his head. "No. We earned it."

## THE INTERNAL SCHISM

Success didn't silence dissent.

Within days of the Athara victory, Lang convened a private gathering of senior partners in an off-site Midtown conference room. The email header read:

*Governance and Guardrails (Confidential)*

When the meeting began, Lang stood before a sleek projection labeled:

*The Case for Controlled Opacity*

He spoke with the precision of a surgeon. "Bill Ellis is redefining transparency as faith. But faith without limits becomes fanaticism. VERITY is overreaching, tracking belief, quantifying contribution, publishing data that should stay sacred. We need a motion for pause."

A few partners nodded. Others hesitated.

Lang pressed harder. "VERITY's idealism will cost us clients. Corporations don't hire confessors—they hire fixers. Erebus may lack soul, but it delivers certainty. We are selling conscience in a market that rewards control."

A partner from London raised her hand. "And what happens when control collapses under its own speed?"

Lang's jaw tensed. "Then we pivot. Quietly. Without sermons."

He knew Bill's strength was moral momentum. His plan was to divide it—to fracture belief before it hardened into culture.

That night, a memo began circulating through private inboxes. Its title:

*The Lang Doctrine: Responsible Opacity in an Era of Radical Transparency.*

It argued for limits on data visibility, for a moratorium on public belief scores, for a return to "executive discretion."

The next morning, Bill found a printed copy on his desk. Someone had underlined a passage:

*Transparency must serve performance, not penance.*

He smiled grimly. Lang had finally declared his war.

## THE RECKONING

That night, Bill sat alone in the darkened boardroom. Outside, Manhattan shimmered like circuitry.

He opened his notebook.

*Belief spreads So does cynicism.*
*Transparency without trust turns into theater.*
*Technology speeds everything up, including the rot.*

He stared at the last line.

Maybe Lang was right about one thing: belief without governance is chaos.

He wrote:

*We need an ethics of judgment.*

Below it, he sketched the outline of a new council—diverse, cross-disciplinary, empowered to question not the code but the conscience behind it. The firm's first Council on Judgment and Integrity.

He underlined the name twice.

## THE PULSE

Weeks later, VERITY's network map stretched across time zones like a band of light across time zones, alive, adjusting, and still learning.

In São Paulo, a young analyst logged her first contribution. In London, a senior partner uploaded a failure story instead of a win. In Singapore, someone wrote a single line in the Belief Index:

*We're learning how to learn again.*

At midnight, the Courage Chime sounded once in The Lab—a soft, clear note that lingered in the air.

Bill heard it from the hallway, paused, and smiled.

He whispered, "That's what progress sounds like."

Then, in the quiet that followed, he added the words that would open his next chapter—part reflection, part prophecy:

*We built a mirror, and for the first time, we didn't look away.*

MARK VAN SUMEREN

# CHAPTER 7

# The Council

Morning arrived brittle and pale, the kind of New York winter light that made even glass look tired. Bill Ellis sat alone in his office, staring at the scrawled words from the night before.

*Council on Judgment and Integrity*

He rolled the phrase across his mind like a stone in his hand, rough, imperfect, grounding. It wasn't strategy; it was something older, something closer to conscience.

VERITY had changed everything. Too fast. Too completely. It had made the invisible visible, and visibility frightened people.

He turned his chair toward the window. Down below, Bryant Park was a wash of gray and breath. Somewhere, beneath layers of concrete and ambition, the city's heart kept time with the servers humming in The Lab two floors beneath him.

He picked up his phone and sent a message to Robert Gaines:

*Need one hour with the Management Committee. Today.*

The reply came two minutes later.

*Make it nine. They're restless.*

Bill smiled grimly. "So am I."

## THE MEETING

The boardroom was already full when he arrived. Robert stood by the screen, arms crossed, while partners murmured in clusters, voices like static, too many frequencies at once.

Edward Lang sat near the center, immaculate as always, his notes arranged with surgical symmetry.

Bill took his place at the head of the table and waited for the noise to fade.

"Let's start," he said simply.

Robert gestured to the display. "VERITY's impact report," he said. "Engagement is up 200%. Client renewals up nine points. But so is partner anxiety. People are calling it 'Ellis's Panopticon.'"

A few quiet chuckles.

Bill nodded. "Fear's just the bill that shows up whenever you try to change anything. But if we want the dividend, we must earn it."

He let that sit, then clicked to a blank slide.

"This isn't about the numbers today. This is about what kind of firm we want to be."

Lang leaned back. "Always dangerous ground for a consultancy."

"Necessary ground," Bill said. "We've built a system that learns from our best and our worst. If we don't govern it with some integrity, it will pick up our shortcuts just as quickly as our strengths."

He turned to the group.

"I'm forming a Council on Judgment and Integrity — an independent body of partners, analysts, clients, and external voices who will define the moral framework for our AI and our firm. Their job isn't to slow us down; it's to make sure we don't forget what we're doing this for."

Lang's expression sharpened. "So now we're hiring philosophers?"

"Yes," Bill said. "And ethicists. And clients. And maybe even a poet or two."

Laughter rippled, thin but real.

Robert studied him carefully. "And the Council reports to…?"

Bill smiled. "The truth. Failing that, to me."

The room stirred — admiration from some, unease from others.

Lang folded his hands. "You're turning conscience into a department, Bill. Noble, sure. Also, naïve."

"No," Bill said firmly. "It's overdue."

## AFTERMATH

After the meeting, the firm split along invisible lines. You could feel it in the elevators, in the tone of emails, in the rhythm of hallway conversations.

Some partners saw the Council as salvation. Others saw it as surveillance in moral clothing.

Lang's allies, now quietly numerous, began whispering about "Ellis's theology of transparency." They spoke of "governance creep" and "strategic overreach."

A memo circulated that afternoon from Lang's office:

*Subject: Preserving Operational Clarity*

*In light of recent initiatives, the Management Committee should reaffirm that ethical oversight must serve, not supplant, commercial judgment.*

Bill read it and smiled. Lang was predictable, but so, once, had been the markets.

## THE ARCHITECTS

The Council on Judgment and Integrity was never meant to be a committee of titles. Bill didn't want hierarchy, politics, or posturing. He wanted conscience. He wanted people who would say the quiet truth out loud. People unawed by power or proximity. People who couldn't be bribed by speed, who were suspicious of groupthink.

He chose them for independence, not influence. For their willingness to see what others missed, and to say what others avoided. Judgment, he knew, lived at the edges, not at the top of the org chart.

AI didn't care about titles. Judgment didn't either. Bill wanted the people who could see around corners, not the people who signed expense reports.

By Friday, the Council's founding members gathered in The Lab - six people chosen not for seniority but for temperament.

*Gretchen Wolfe* was restless, almost relentless. The antibody against complacency. She refuses easy answers and pushes past politeness. She doesn't confuse consensus with correctness. Her restlessness is her authority; it keeps the Council from drifting into comfort.

*Samir Patel* was the architect of VERITY's logic. He understood the inner workings of the firm's most consequential technology. He knew where bias could hide and where values could warp. He also knew when a technical decision quietly turned into an ethical one. He was the bridge between intention and implementation, the one who spotted risks leadership couldn't see.

*Tracy Prefontaine* was skeptical and surgical. She represented disciplined dissent. Tracy was built for cutting through narratives and corporate mythologies, for slicing away wishful thinking. Her skepticism wasn't cynicism; it was precision. The Council needed someone who could perform conceptual surgery.

*Angela Chen*, the client representative, was sharp as wire. A Council about judgment, she argued, couldn't be inward-looking. Angela brought the voice of those who felt the consequences of the firm's decisions. She was sharp and unfiltered, and she didn't have to care about internal politics. She reminded the Council that ethics wasn't a branding exercise; it was something clients could feel.

*Dr. Harlan Cho*, a philosopher from Columbia University, specialized in machine ethics. He grounded the Council in first principles and wasn't clouded by revenue targets or timelines.

His authority came from perspective, from the ability to frame questions others didn't know to ask. Philosophers weren't mid-level, he liked to say. They were structural. They challenged assumptions the rest of the Council was too close to see.

*Leah Owens*, a journalist Bill trusted enough to fear, represented public accountability. She wasn't there to protect the firm; she was there to expose it if she had to. Her presence forced transparency and a different kind of discipline. When someone in the room could write the headline, everyone behaved differently. That was the point.

They weren't the most powerful people in the firm. They were just the ones least willing to lie to themselves.

Bill opened the Council's first meeting with a single sentence: "Every revolution needs its conscience."

Harlan smiled faintly. "And its humility."

Samir projected VERITY's core schema on the wall, a map of connections glowing in the dim room.

"This system learns from everything we feed it," he said. "That's its power. And its danger."

Gretchen added, "If we don't filter for intent, we'll just automate our own biases."

Angela nodded. "And if we filter too tightly, we'll neuter the thing that makes us competitive."

Bill said nothing for a long time. He was watching VERITY's nodes shimmer like thoughts.

"Let's not confuse conscience with handcuffs," he said finally. "I don't care if the machine sounds polite. I care that it's honest."

Leah, ever the reporter, asked, "And who decides what's honest?"

Bill looked up. "We do. Together and out loud. That's the work."

## LANG'S GAMBIT

The following week, Lang made his move.

A leak, subtle and surgical, appeared in The Financial Chronicle:

*Inside the AI Panic at Barney-Hamilton: Partners Divided Over 'Ethics Council.' Critics warn of moral bureaucracy as firm faces Erebus Labs' accelerating advantage.*

The article quoted "an anonymous senior partner" describing VERITY as "a digital confessional for consultants who've lost their edge."

By noon, the firm's PR team was in crisis mode.

Robert stormed into Bill's office. "You've been ambushed. The Street's asking if we're becoming a think tank."

Bill read the article twice, then set it down. "Good. At least they're asking questions again."

"Lang's fingerprints are all over this," Robert said.

"I know," Bill replied. "Let him have the headlines. We'll keep the substance."

## THE COUNCIL'S FIRST TEST

That afternoon, the Council convened for its inaugural session. The agenda was simple: approve the first Ethical Framework for Machine Judgment.

Samir outlined the stakes. "VERITY is starting to suggest actions, not just insights. If we don't draw boundaries, it will optimize for outcomes we never intended."

Harlan adjusted his glasses. "Then the first rule should be humility: every recommendation must include its uncertainty."

Angela countered. "Clients pay for confidence, not caveats."

"Clients pay for consequences," Tracy said. "They just forget that part until later."

The debate sharpened. Voices overlapped. Philosophy collided with profit.

Bill let it unfold. He wanted the friction.

Finally, he raised a hand. "Here's the line," he said. "Every algorithm must show its reasoning. Every output must name its assumptions. And every recommendation must be traceable to a human accountable for its interpretation."

Leah tapped her pen. "A conscience clause for machines."

"Exactly," Bill said. "We're not going to blame the system. If it recommends something, a human signs their name under it."

The motion passed unanimously.

## THE HEARING

Two days later, Lang called for a Management Committee "review" of the Council's authority. It was theater, of course, and it was well-scripted.

The boardroom was packed. The air felt thick, like everyone was performing.

Lang began with practiced calm. "We all appreciate Mr. Ellis's commitment to ethics," he said. "But we must ask whether this Council represents governance or overreach. Our clients hire us for clarity, not catechism."

Bill let him finish.

Then he spoke, voice low but steady. "You're right, Edward. Clients hire us for clarity. But clarity without conscience is just precision in the wrong direction. You can have speed, or you can have stewardship. We choose both, but only if we remember which one matters first."

Lang leaned forward. "And who decides what matters?"

Bill smiled. "The people willing to take responsibility for it. The rest can stay spectators."

Murmurs. Silence. Then, quietly, Robert said, "Motion to endorse the Council as standing governance."

Hands rose — slowly at first, then more confidently.

Lang didn't raise his.

But he didn't walk out, either.

## NIGHT WORK

Later that night, Bill sat alone in The Lab. VERITY glowed softly in the dark. Its filaments like veins of thought.

He could see new nodes forming: reflections, debates, small confessions from analysts halfway around the world.

One caught his eye:

> *I used to think AI would replace me. Now I think it's teaching me*
> *how to think again.*

He smiled, tired and proud.

Tracy appeared in the doorway. "Lang won't stop," she said.

"I know."

"He's building a shadow group, the 'Pragmatics.' Quiet, loyal, scared. They'll push for a merger or a sale."

Bill rubbed his temples. "There's always capital for fear. There's never a shortage of people willing to bet on panic."

"What's our move?"

"Keep building belief," he said. "It's the only currency that compounds."

## THE COLLAPSE OF CERTAINTY

Two weeks later, the unexpected happened.

Erebus failed.

A multinational energy client that had relied exclusively on Erebus's predictive models suffered a $1.2 billion misstep when the algorithm misread geopolitical variables and triggered a supply-chain implosion.

The story hit every major paper:

> *When AI Overreaches: Erebus Error Costs Titan Energy*
> *Billions.*

Suddenly, Barney-Hamilton's approach — measured, ethical, transparent — looked prophetic.

Clients and journalists called, curious about the firm's renewed competitiveness. Investors re-doubled their interest in acquiring Barney-Hamilton or, at least, securing a stake in the business.

Robert burst into Bill's office, grinning like a man remembering how to breathe. "You've been vindicated!"

Bill shook his head. "No. Just reminded that machines don't stop us from making human mistakes. They just let us make them at scale."

He stared out the window. "Now we prove we can do better."

## THE COUNCIL'S DECLARATION

Three days later, the Council issued its first formal statement:

> *The Charter of Judgment and Integrity*
> *Every model must reveal its reasoning.*
> *Every algorithm must name its blind spots.*
> *Every decision must trace to a human owner.*
> *Belief and accountability are indivisible.*
> *Transparency is not the absence of privacy; it's the presence of courage.*

The Charter concluded with a final clause that would come to define the firm's philosophy on artificial intelligence:

> *Business intelligence, unlike artificial intelligence, derives its value not from computation but from conscience. Thus, its effectiveness rests on four conditions governing the responsible use of artificial intelligence: the quality of the data that shapes it, the precision of the questions posed to it, the human values that constrain it, and the professional judgment applied to it. Machines accelerate thought; only humans ensure that thought means something.*

It was concise, almost mathematical, yet deeply moral, a compact between technology and those entrusted to wield it.

It was signed by all six Council members — and, quietly, by Robert Gaines. Within days, the Management Committee formally endorsed the Charter.

Lang did not sign. But he didn't block it either.

That evening, VERITY displayed the Charter on every screen for exactly one minute, framed by the words:

> *Judgment is the new intelligence.*

## PRIVATE REFLECTIONS

That night, Bill called Sarah Kim in Ann Arbor. She answered on the second ring.

"I read the Charter," she said. "You sound like a man trying to rebuild the Church."

"I'm trying to rebuild trust."

She laughed softly. "Same thing, different hymns."

The Judgment Studios had become the modern heirs of the Design Shops — the Taylors' great experiment in collective insight reborn through technology. What had once been walls covered in paper was now a living network of data and discourse. Yet the purpose endured: to make collaboration visible, and to make intelligence accountable.

He looked out at the city, lights flickering like neurons. "Do you ever wonder if we're just buying time before the machines learn morality faster than we can?"

"No," she said. "Because morality isn't a function. It's a choice. And choice doesn't scale."

He closed his eyes. "Then maybe that's what we sell now — the courage to choose."

"Then sell it," she said. "Before someone else automates it."

## CODA: THE COUNCIL ROOM

Weeks later, the Council's new chamber opened — a circular room lined with glass and history. On the wall behind Bill's chair, etched into steel, was the Charter.

He looked around the table — Gretchen, Samir, Tracy, Angela, Harlan, Leah — each worn but luminous in their own way.

"Today," he said, "we stop being a consulting firm and start being something rarer — a place where judgment has a home."

Samir smiled faintly. "You know what they'll say?"

"What?"

"That we've gone soft."

Bill looked at VERITY glowing through the glass wall, a slow pulse, alive, learning.

"Then let them," he said. "Soft things bend. Rigid ones break."

The Courage Chime sounded once — clear, steady.

The room fell silent.

Bill opened his notebook and wrote:

> *Integrity is just intelligence that remembers what it promised last time.*

He underlined it once, closed the book, and looked up.

Outside, the city pulsed — bright, brittle, becoming something new.

Inside, for the first time in a long time, the firm felt alive.

MARK VAN SUMEREN

# CHAPTER 8

# The Reckoning of Lang

It didn't arrive with a coup. It started with a whisper.

At first, Bill Ellis mistook it for static, the kind of low institutional hum that always accompanied success. The firm was thriving again. VERITY's integration with client systems had begun to redefine what consulting looked like. Barney-Hamilton was no longer a collection of thinkers selling slides; it had become a living network of judgment and learning.

But beneath the optimism, something else was moving, quiet, organized, and just patient enough to be dangerous.

The Pragmatics.

Lang's faction.

They considered themselves realists. They met after hours, sometimes offsite, sometimes in encrypted video calls with names like "Governance Planning Session" or "Client Sustainability Forum." The titles were harmless. The intent was not.

By the time Bill heard the first rumor, they already had a plan.

## THE LEAK

It surfaced on a Monday morning in April, the kind of morning when the city felt newly thawed, its streets shining with dirty meltwater and fresh ambition.

Robert Gaines entered Bill's office without knocking, carrying a printout that looked like it had been crumpled in anger.

"They leaked the client data framework," Robert said, his voice taut.

Bill looked up from his notes. "Which one?"

"The Athara engagement. Erebus Labs just announced a 'joint optimization study' with Titan Bio. They used our proprietary VERITY schema — word for word."

Bill's stomach sank. "That framework was locked."

"Apparently not. Someone in London exported it two nights ago."

"Another Marcus Levy?"

Robert shook his head. "Worse. A partner with senior clearance."

Bill's first instinct wasn't rage. It was silence, and then calculation. "Lang," he said quietly.

Robert hesitated. "We can't prove it yet."

Bill leaned back, staring at the ceiling. "Then let's not waste time proving. Let's start preventing."

## THE COUNCIL CONVENES

By afternoon, the Council on Judgment and Integrity assembled in The Lab. The mood was darker than usual. VERITY's glow looked colder, the Courage Chime stayed quiet.

Gretchen spoke first. "If the Pragmatics are leaking frameworks, this isn't dissent. It's sabotage."

Tracy nodded. "They're betting the firm will flinch before it fights. Classic insurgent logic."

Samir was staring at a schematic of VERITY's access logs. "They're not wrong. The permissions tree still gives senior partners carte blanche. It's legacy code from the old world."

"Then rewrite the world," Bill said.

Angela frowned. "That means suspending partner privileges. You'll start a civil war."

"That started a while ago," Bill said. "We just haven't called it one."

Harlan Cho, the philosopher, leaned forward. "A question: are we protecting data, or protecting belief?"

Bill looked at him. "Both. Because if they steal our frameworks, we can rebuild them. But if they steal our faith, we're done."

## LANG'S RETURN

Lang didn't hide. He walked into the boardroom the next day wrapped in his usual, practiced confidence, like nothing had shifted.

"Edward," Bill said, smiling without warmth. "You're staging a coup."

Bill gestured toward a chair. "Sit. Tell me about the leak."

Lang's eyebrows lifted. "You think I'd risk my career over a file?"

"I think you'd risk anything to prove a point."

Lang sat. "Then let me make it plainly. The Council has become a liability. Clients love the ethics talk until it slows their profits. Our own partners are suffocating under belief metrics and contribution ledgers. Erebus offers them autonomy. You offer them confession."

Bill's voice stayed calm. "You call it confession. I call it clarity."

Lang's eyes hardened. "Clarity doesn't pay bonuses."

"It pays longevity."

Lang leaned in. "You've turned a consulting firm into a monastery. You're asking capitalists to worship courage. That won't last."

"Then let's see which one history remembers," Bill said quietly.

Lang stood, buttoned his jacket, and smiled like a man certain of his checkmate. "You've mistaken leadership for faith, Bill. The firm deserves something steadier."

## THE VOTE

Three days later, the Management Committee called an emergency session.

*Agenda: Motion to Review Governance Structure and Council Authority*

In plain terms: a challenge to the Council's legitimacy.

The bankers were circling. Ardent Capital had quietly increased its bid to $1.295 billion, sweetening the deal with retention bonuses and a liquidity window for senior partners.

The conversations in the halls had changed. Partners no longer debated values; they calculated multiples. Ardent Capital had begun reaching out through intermediaries, testing sentiment. Lang had taken one of those calls, just to listen—or so he said.

"They're serious players," he mentioned casually in a meeting. Bill caught the flicker of something, respect, maybe ambition. Armitage was smart enough not to call Lang directly again, but the message was clear: the offer stood.

Bill received a message through a third-party advisor. "No pressure," Armitage's voice had purred, "but these windows don't stay open long."

The timing was surgical: one day before the vote.

Twenty-four partners sat around the table. No assistants. No observers. The blinds were half-drawn, muting the morning light into a dull gray wash across the wood.

Lang watched the room settle into its ritual silence, the same choreography he had once commanded with ease. But this morning, the stillness didn't answer to him. Beneath his calm exterior, a pulse of panic whispered: if belief replaced hierarchy, what place was left for a man whose authority came from structure?

Jackets stayed on. Coffee cooled. The air felt close, expectant.

Robert opened. "We'll hear both sides. No interruptions."

Lang spoke first. He was magnificent, polished, poised, lethal.

He talked about markets and efficiency, about fiduciary duty. He spoke of "existential overreach" and "the drift from client focus to moral theater." He quoted statutes and cited margins, and somehow made ethics sound like inefficiency.

When he finished, silence. The kind that meant assent. A few heads inclined. Eyes stayed down.

Bill rose. The chair legs whispered against the floor. No slides or notes. Just a folded legal pad.

"I respect Edward Lang," he said. "He's brilliant. Disciplined. And wrong."

He waited, letting the words settle.

"When we built VERITY, we didn't invent technology, we remembered humanity. We stopped pretending intelligence was scarce and realized judgment was. That became our advantage."

He looked around the table, slowly and deliberately.

"Lang talks about efficiency. Fair point. But efficiency without trust is just speed, and speed kills companies faster than failure."

A chair creaked. Someone shifted.

"Our clients don't come to us because we're fast," Bill continued. "They come because when every other firm asks, 'What's legal?' we ask, 'What's right?' That's our brand. That's our margin. And that's what's at stake here."

He paused. "Edward believes profit will save us. I believe purpose protects profit. That isn't sentiment. It's discipline.

Look at the firms that forgot it — dismantled, sold off, absorbed by those that still stand for something."

Then, quieter: "You're right about risk, Edward. You're just measuring the wrong kind."

The silence wasn't polite anymore. It was focused, alive.

Bill's voice softened. "We can live with either belief. But only one survives contact with the future."

He sat. The chair creaked once and stilled. No one moved.

Robert cleared his throat. "We'll vote."

Hands rose, deliberate and weighted. He counted twice before looking up.

For the motion: 10. Against: 14.

A collective breath. Robert nodded. "The motion fails. The Council stands."

Lang blinked once, still composed. Then gave a small, professional nod.

He'd spent his life mastering the art of composure, but in that quiet nod was the smallest confession—that control, once lost, cannot be rebuilt through dignity alone. The vote hadn't just defeated his motion; it had exiled his certainty.

Chairs pushed back and the Committee members stood, gathering their papers.. The hum of restraint returned.

Bill stayed seated a moment longer, the echo of the vote still in the air. Not victory. Not triumph. Just relief, the quiet kind that comes when a company remembers what it is.

## FALLOUT

The next morning, Lang's resignation letter hit the firmwide inbox.

> *Effective immediately, I am stepping down as Senior Partner of Barney-Hamilton & Co. I believe the firm's future lies not in reflection but in performance. I wish you well in your pursuit of conscience.*

An hour later, the news broke. Lang and key partners join Erebus Labs to form "Erebus Advisory."

The market exploded. Clients called. Competitors whispered to each other in cautious tones.

With Lang's exit, the question of selling to Ardent—or licensing VERITY's IP—died as abruptly as it had surfaced. Without him to drive it, no one dared revive the conversation. The proposal had always been his crusade, the easy answer for partners who mistook liquidity for legacy. In its silence, the firm found something unexpected: relief. The idea of monetizing VERITY no longer seemed strategic; it seemed sacrilegious.

Robert found Bill in his office, staring at the headline.

"You lost half the room," Robert said.

"I lost the ones who forgot what room they were in," Bill replied.

## THE CRISIS

The first week after the defection was chaos. Clients froze contracts and recruiters circled like vultures.

Lang's new firm positioned itself as the "anti-Barney-Hamilton": fast, decisive, algorithmic. Their slogan was everywhere:

*Decisions Without Doubt*

It was a smart shot at Bill's slower, more reflective model.

Inside Barney-Hamilton, morale wavered. The Belief Index dipped. The Courage Chime stayed silent for three days.

Gretchen stormed into Bill's office. "We're bleeding clients. Everyone's second-guessing. Lang's promising results in half the time. He's using our playbook!"

Bill closed his eyes. "He's using our plays. He just doesn't have the soul that wrote them."

Tracy crossed her arms. "Soul doesn't pay invoices."

He looked up, exhausted but steady. "Neither does panic."

He stood, walked to the window, and whispered,

*Believing is hard. Remembering why you started might be harder.*

## THE CALL

That evening, Bill's phone rang. Angela Chen.

"I've just been pitched by Erebus Advisory," she said. "They're offering to replicate your VERITY insights for a fraction of the cost."

Bill said nothing.

Angela continued. "They say judgment is overrated. That clients need certainty, not sermons."

He smiled faintly. "They're half right. Clients need courage — and courage is never certain."

There was silence on the line.

Then she said, "You know what's funny? I don't believe them. Erebus feels... hollow. All speed, no soul."

"Then stay," Bill said softly. "Help us prove that humanity scales."

She laughed. "You always know how to make stubborn sound noble."

## THE LONG NIGHT

That night, The Lab stayed lit past midnight. VERITY glowed brighter than usual and drew analysts like moths.

Samir was rewriting access protocols. Gretchen was onboarding new data safeguards. Tracy was reworking the Belief Index into something deeper, a Trust Map that traced not just sentiment but behavior.

Bill walked among them quietly, feeling the hum of purpose returning.

He paused by the whiteboard, still covered in half-erased equations. In one corner, someone had scrawled:

*People remember who they are when it starts to hurt.*

He touched the words with his fingertips. "We will," he whispered.

## LANG'S STRIKE

Alone in his new office at Erebus Advisory, Lang sat in senior-partner luxury: thick carpet, framed art, curated silence. The room still felt colder than the hallways he'd walked to reach it. He'd expected exhilaration but found only static. Erebus Advisory moved fast, too fast, and he began to miss the weight of reflection he once mocked.

He drafted the open letter - part defiance, part plea. A way to prove, mostly to himself, he still mattered to the argument.

Two days later, he struck.

Erebus Advisory released Lang's open letter in The Wall Street Journal:

*Barney-Hamilton's obsession with belief is a distraction from performance. Judgment without velocity is nostalgia. We choose precision over poetry.*

The line went viral in corporate circles.

But it also sparked something unexpected.

A countertrend.

*#JudgmentOverVelocity* began trending on professional networks; a quiet rebellion among executives tired of automation masquerading as wisdom.

Bill watched the debate unfold and smiled. "He just handed us our tagline," he said.

## THE RECKONING

Three months later, Erebus Advisory's recklessness caught up with them.

A global conglomerate, Helion Foods, sued for breach of fiduciary duty after an Erebus-driven strategy collapsed spectacularly. The algorithms had optimized profits by cutting quality controls, resulting in contaminated product lines.

The scandal was everywhere.

*When Algorithms Forget Ethics.*

*Erebus Advisory: Intelligence Without Integrity.*

Lang's picture was on the cover of Fortune. He looked older already.

Robert entered Bill's office holding the magazine. "He's finished."

Bill shook his head. "No. He's teaching the world what happens when speed forgets meaning."

## THE RETURN

Weeks later, an email arrived.

> From: Edward Lang
> Subject: No Subject
> Bill,
> You were right.
> We built a machine that never doubted, and it devoured us.
> If the Council still exists, tell it this: doubt is not

weakness. It's the first sign of wisdom.

—E.

Bill read it twice. Then a third time.

The words were brittle but honest, the kind a man writes when ambition finally meets conscience. Lang's brilliance had never been in question, only his fear of fading into the background of the machine he once commanded. In that final line, he gave Bill what he could never give himself: permission to doubt.

He closed his eyes. "Welcome back, Edward," he whispered.

## AFTERLIGHT

Months passed. The firm healed, slowly at first, then all at once.

VERITY became not just a tool but a conscience. It began surfacing questions instead of answers. Under the Council's guidance, it started to suggest context more than conclusions. VERITY learned to frame truth as a question, not to test intelligence, but to teach care.

Clients noticed. Trust returned.

And somewhere, in a quiet office in Brooklyn, Edward Lang began advising nonprofits on ethical governance of AI.

Gretchen found the article first and showed Bill.

He smiled faintly. "Even cynics can evolve."

## THE RECKONING WITHIN

That night, alone in The Lab, Bill opened his notebook, the same leather-bound journal that had followed him from Ann Arbor to every boardroom battle.

He wrote slowly, deliberately:

> *We built VERITY to make machines human.*
> *In the end, it made us human again.*
>
> *Judgment isn't certainty about what's right.*
> *It's the decision to keep asking, even when you'd rather be done.*

He closed the notebook, turned off the lights, and listened as the Courage Chime sounded once, low, clear, infinite.

Outside, the city glowed like circuitry against the night. Every window felt like a story. Every light, a memory.

And inside, one man finally exhaled, not in victory, but in peace.

MARK VAN SUMEREN

CHAPTER 9

# The Renewal

It was spring again in New York: tentative, damp, reluctant.

The trees along Bryant Park stood in hesitant green, and the city had begun to hum with that optimism it reserves for April. In the Barney-Hamilton tower, sunlight finally reached the upper floors, spilling across glass and steel like the promise of forgiveness.

Bill Ellis stood by his window, hands in his pockets, watching the street below. The traffic moved with the same purpose it always had, but somehow the noise seemed gentler. Or maybe, he thought, it was him who had changed.

On his desk lay a letter, hand-signed on thick stationery. The top read:

> *Barney-Hamilton Council on Judgment and Integrity*
> *Subject: Transition Proposal*

He'd written the letter himself, three days earlier, and still hadn't sent it.

## THE BRIEFING

The day began with a leadership briefing. Council members filled the glass conference room, Bill, Gretchen, Samir, Tracy, Angela, Harlon, and Leah.

VERITY now served as the Council's silent eighth member, its surface alive with faint ripples of color, like breath moving beneath glass.

Robert and the firm's Management Committee filed in a few minutes later.

Gretchen opened. "We've finalized integration with three Fortune 50 clients. VERITY's hybrid AI-human framework is being cited as an industry model."

Samir added, "We've also released the 'Ethical Learning Core.' It ensures our algorithms adapt from verified cases only — no data scrapes, no noise."

Bill nodded. "Quality over quantity. We finally built a memory worth trusting."

Tracy smirked. "We're the only firm that sells judgment as a service and means it."

Robert smiled, his eyes weary but proud. "You realize, don't you, that we've done what no one thought possible — we made ethics profitable."

"Not ethics," Bill said softly. "Integrity. Ethics are rules. Integrity is behavior when no one's looking."

## A VISIT FROM MICHIGAN

That afternoon, Bill's assistant knocked at his office door. "You have a visitor," she said. "From Ann Arbor."

Bill turned, startled. "Send her in."

Sarah Kim entered, her coat still dusted with rain, the same calm intelligence in her eyes that had once helped him find balance in the storm.

"I was in town for a symposium," she said. "I thought I'd see if the philosopher-CEO still keeps office hours."

He smiled. "Barely. These days, I'm more curator than commander, and honestly, that feels right"

They sat by the window. For a while, they didn't speak. They didn't need to.

Finally, she said, "You've changed the conversation, Bill. People don't ask if AI will replace them anymore. They ask how to become irreplaceable beside it."

He nodded. "That was always the point. Machines can replicate thought, not wisdom."

"And Lang?"

Bill smiled faintly. "He's teaching again. Ethics for Engineers at NYU. Calls it 'The Practice of Doubt.' I sent him a bottle of bourbon."

Sarah laughed softly. "You've both grown up."

"Or just grown tired," he said.

"Same thing sometimes."

## THE NEXT GENERATION

Later that week, Bill hosted a session with the firm's youngest associates, twenty of them, bright-eyed and sharp, born into a world where tools like Erebus and VERITY were as ordinary as calculators.

He began with a story.

"When I joined Barney-Hamilton," he said, "we thought intelligence was the currency of success. The smartest idea won. But intelligence is easy now. Machines have that in surplus. What's rare is courage — the courage to ask better questions, to hold judgment long enough to find the truth, to care when caring costs something."

A young consultant raised her hand. "Do you think AI will ever outgrow us?"

Bill smiled. "I hope so. And if it does, I hope it learns humility faster than we did."

Another asked, "So what's our role now?"

"Meaning," he said simply. "We translate data into meaning. That's leadership in the age of intelligence: finding what matters when everything is measurable."

## THE TRANSITION

By June, the Council had evolved into something larger, an international consortium of firms, universities, and civic institutions. What began as Barney-Hamilton's conscience had become the industry's compass.

Robert approached him one evening, hands in pockets. "They want you to chair the consortium," he said.

Bill looked out at the city's amber dusk. "No. It's time for someone new. Someone who believes in the system without being trapped by its history."

"Gretchen?" Robert asked.

Bill nodded. "She's ready. She has the fire, and she has patience. That's rarer than genius."

Robert was quiet for a moment. "Are you sure you're ready to step aside?"

Bill smiled. "I'm not stepping aside. I'm stepping back, where the view's clearer."

## THE FINAL COUNCIL

The Council gathered one last time under Bill's chairmanship.

The room was quiet, sunlight filtering through the glass. On the screen behind them glowed VERITY's updated interface — sleek, intuitive, almost human in its responsiveness.

Gretchen spoke first. "Before we begin, I want to acknowledge something. None of this: the Council, VERITY, the culture, exists without you, Bill."

He shook his head. "It exists because we needed it. I just gave it a name."

Tracy added, "You gave it a heart."

Samir smiled. "And enough curiosity to survive our mistakes."

Bill looked around the table at the people who had walked through doubt and come out stronger.

He said quietly, "We built a mirror, and this time, we didn't look away. That's the part that matters. Don't let it fog over."

Then he signed the document transferring the Council's chairmanship to Gretchen Wolfe.

The Courage Chime sounded once.

## RETURN TO ANN ARBOR

A month later, Bill stood on the sidelines of Michigan Stadium, the late summer air heavy with nostalgia.

The scoreboard still glinted like armor in the sunlight. A group of student-athletes ran drills on the turf, their movements sharp, disciplined, joyful.

An assistant athletic director approached him. "Glad you came back, Bill. You helped us rethink NIL when everyone else was just chasing dollars."

Bill smiled. "Turns out, belief scales there too."

As he watched the players run the "Michigan Drill," he thought about the parallels, of how both worlds had learned to merge tradition with transformation.

He pulled a folded page from his jacket pocket. On it, a line from his old notebook:

*Those who stay will be champions.*

He whispered, "Still true."

## LEGACY

Back in New York, Barney-Hamilton continued to evolve. VERITY had become something far larger, a living archive of human and machine wisdom intertwined.

The firm no longer billed by the hour. It billed by impact: measurable improvements in sustainable outcomes, and in the trust renewed between client and advisor.

AI was everywhere now, but Barney-Hamilton's moat remained: its proprietary data, its curated memory, its living culture of judgment.

Competitors could copy the tools. What they never seemed to manage was the soul.

## THE QUIET ENDING

One evening, long after the office had emptied, Bill returned to The Lab.

VERITY glowed softly in the dark, its surface pulsing with faint, rhythmic light — the heartbeat of an organization learning how to feel.

He rested a hand on the glass. The surface brightened under his palm, a soft tone sounded, and VERITY's almost-human voice filled the empty Lab.

"Hello, Bill," it said. "Would you like to reflect today?"

He smiled. "Just once more."

There was a brief pause, like the system was taking a breath.

"Go ahead," VERITY replied. "I'm listening."

Bill looked out at the darkened city, then back at the slow pulse of light beneath his hand.

"Leadership isn't about knowing the future," he said. "It's acting like we can be ready for whatever shows up."

For a moment, only the quiet hum of the servers answered him.

Then VERITY's voice returned, softer now. "Thank you, old friend."

The light along the glass deepened, a single steady glow.

"We remember," it said.

He stood there for a long moment, hand still on the panel, watching the glow fade slowly into darkness.

Then he turned off the lights and walked out. The building kept humming behind him, not ending so much as continuing without him.

# The Next Game

The sky over Ann Arbor was a perfect late-fall blue: cold and brittle, sharp enough to make you feel awake just by breathing it. The streets were lined with banners, the kind that carried both history and hope:

*Go Blue*
*Leaders and Best*

Bill Ellis walked slowly toward Michigan Stadium, his scarf pulled tight, the air curling from his breath like smoke. It had been almost three years since he scribbled the words in the margin:

*Legacy without renewal dies.*

Now, as he crossed the concourse into a sea of maize and blue, he realized that the line had become something more than a note in a margin. It was the story of his life, and of every institution that forgot how to learn until it almost disappeared.

VERITY had gone live six months ago. Not the prototype, not the pilot — the real system running in the wild. At first, people had feared it would replace them. Then they realized it simply reflected them — sharper, faster, and sometimes uncomfortably honest.

Every morning, VERITY pulsed with the rhythm of the firm's collective mind. Belief scores rose and fell like weather. The Courage Chime rang across offices in London, Singapore, and New York — a faint, melodic heartbeat that reminded them all why they worked. The system didn't just process data anymore; it gave context shape. It learned something about what made courage contagious.

And sometimes, Bill thought, it reacted in ways that felt uncomfortably human.

The week before, Gretchen had shown him something odd in VERITY's interaction logs. When asked why a decision mattered, the system had started weighting responses that contained words like trust, care, and belief more heavily than those that referenced margin, velocity, or market share.

"It's learning what we value," Gretchen had said.

Bill smiled at the memory. "Or reminding us what we forgot."

He'd written in his notebook that night:

> *The first intelligence revolution ended the day we started pretending machines could think for us. The next would only start if they ever helped us feel again.*

Now, in the crisp brightness of game day, the roar of the crowd swelled through the concrete. He climbed the stadium steps and emerged into sunlight and noise — a living cathedral of tradition. More than a hundred thousand people stood together, singing the fight song as if it could will a championship back into existence.

On the jumbotron, the broadcast panned over the student section. Behind him, someone shouted, "Go Blue!" and another voice answered, "Beat Ohio!"

Bill found his seat. He chose the bowl instead of his suite. He wanted to feel the crowd, not simply observe it from behind the glass.

His phone buzzed. A message from Gretchen lit the screen:

> *VERITY update: Belief Index at 93%. Firm-wide. Unprecedented.*

He smiled — not because the number was high, but because it had been earned. Every point of belief represented a conversation repaired, a culture revived, a leader choosing renewal over resignation.

The announcer's voice boomed through the stadium. The teams lined up. For a moment, time folded. He could almost see the parallels: the firm and the field, the players and the partners, both trying to prove that tradition and innovation could coexist without one consuming the other.

He looked out at the team, at their unity and focus, at the shared pulse running through them. He thought of Barney-Hamilton's new rhythm, human minds working beside machines, not beneath them. Belief measured not by surveys, but by courage in action.

As the players ran beneath the banner, the pre-recorded video clip of Bo Schembechler preached the mantra that had defined generations:

*The team, the team, the team.*

Bill, and 107,000 others, repeated it in unison along with Schembechler.

In that instant, he understood something simple and vast: VERITY hadn't replaced leadership, it had resurrected it. Erebus had shown what data could do. VERITY showed what people had to grow into.

He closed his eyes and let the sound of the crowd wash over him — a wave of purpose, history, and renewal. Somewhere in New York, a chime rang softly through the firm's global network: another act of mentorship logged, another question asked better than before.

Bill Ellis smiled, his heart steady, his breath even. The work would continue long after him. That, he realized, was the point.

He reached into his pocket and touched the worn edge of an old Post-it note he still carried, the one he'd found on the floor of The Lab that first night:

*Maybe we're not done.*

He whispered to himself, barely audible beneath the roar:
"Not even close."

MARK VAN SUMEREN

# APPENDICES: Lessons from the Notebooks of Bill Ellis

MARK VAN SUMEREN

# The Architecture of Ownership and Change

Bill Ellis never saw ownership as moral territory. To him, it was just design: the thing that determined who waited, who acted, and who cared. The ownership model sat underneath everything, the part no one talked about, but everyone lived inside. You could reform strategy, hire visionary leaders and invent new tools, but if the ownership model rewarded impatience, the system would relapse the moment the spotlight dimmed.

Private equity, he knew, was the most misunderstood of all ownership forms. To outsiders it seemed predatory. Inside the good firms, it felt more like capital with a backbone. The great private equity firms didn't buy broken companies to gut them; they found sound ones suffocating under their own inertia and gave them air. They provided the capital, the discipline, and the urgency to grow. The worst funds measured victory in months. The best thought in legacies. The difference, he wrote, was intent.

Stone Medical had once depended on such capital. When banks recoiled from risk, it was a quiet, family-backed fund that believed in a ten-year horizon and a simple promise: to restore the company's discipline without amputating its spirit. "They didn't dictate," Bill remembered.

"They breathed life back into the place. They thought in decades, not quarters."

By contrast, the partnership model was a peculiar blend of virtue and vanity. Partnerships always started warm and ended inward. Early on they felt democratic; over time they grew territorial. They rewarded tenure over renewal, continuity over imagination. In their infancy, partnerships felt like democracies of excellence; in their maturity, they hardened into oligarchies of comfort. "A partnership that stops reinvesting stops leading," Bill had written once, "It becomes a pension plan with better stationery." It was the hardest truth to speak to his own partners, but the one that needed saying most.

The public company, for all its accountability, carried its own tyranny. Public markets worshipped precision and punished volatility. CEOs tried to live in two calendars, one measured in quarters, the other in decades, and the effort tore many of them apart. "The market wants predictability." Bill wrote, "Real change needs a little chaos. CEOs get torn between the two." The only way to survive was to keep two clocks running, one for investors and one for innovators. The first demanded evidence; the second demanded faith.

Nonprofits, meanwhile, were the most virtuous and the most paralyzed. Bill admired their missions but pitied their process. Hospitals, universities, and charities all suffered from the same ailment: consensus so sacred it became inertia. "If everyone has veto power," he wrote, "urgency dies on the table." Freedom from shareholders should have made them daring; instead, it made them slow. "Their capital is moral, not financial," he wrote. "Their wealth is virtue, but their debt is time."

Each ownership model had its own allergy to change. Private equity feared uncertainty. Public companies feared disruption. Partnerships feared reinvention. Nonprofits feared conflict. Every one of them worshiped continuity in a world that only rewarded renewal.

He wrote in his notebook,

> *Follow the money and you'll find the clock. Follow the clock and you'll find the culture."*

The longer the clock, the more patience the system could afford. The shorter it was, the more it devoured its own future for the comfort of the present.

If Barney-Hamilton was to survive, its clock would have to be rewound and rebuilt—away from the annual anxiety of partner distributions and toward the compounding patience of purpose.

> *Before we reform the business, we reform the clock. Incentives are the strategy. Everything else is just meeting notes.*

# The Belief Index Framework

The idea for the Belief Index had come to Bill in the quiet hours after his first town hall. He had looked into the eyes of partners, analysts, and assistants and seen something missing—not cynicism, but fatigue. Belief had thinned out. Not all at once, more like a slow leak that nobody noticed. Without belief, no transformation could take hold.

The Belief Index began not as a metric but as a mirror. Bill knew belief couldn't be commanded or coerced. It could only be revealed. "We are not measuring belief to control it," he told the team. "We are measuring it so we can stop pretending."

The framework was deceptively simple: three questions, asked anonymously each month, and the results were published openly.

> *Do you believe Barney-Hamilton makes you better?*
> *Do you believe we make our clients better?*
> *Do you believe we are getting better ourselves?*

The first question tested pride, the second purpose, the third hope.

In the early months, the results were brutal. Scores came back fractured. Analysts trusted the firm more than partners did. Clients believed in individuals more than the institution. Belief had stratified, like silt in a riverbed. But that honesty was the point. "The pretty numbers were lulling us," Bill said. "The ugly ones were the only thing honest enough to get our attention."

Over time, the Index evolved into something larger—a rhythm. Teams began posting their scores on whiteboards beside delivery milestones. VERITY integrated the data, mapping how belief correlated with retention, innovation, and client renewal. The patterns were unmistakable. High-belief teams outperformed low-belief ones by double digits. Cynicism cost us. Trust, oddly enough, paid dividends.

Bill saw in the Index not just morale but strategy.

He wrote,

*Belief moves first. The numbers just catch up later.*

In one meeting, he compared belief to oxygen: invisible, essential, and always the first thing to thin when the air grew cold.

When a skeptical partner asked why any of it mattered, Bill pointed to a wall where a chart showed belief rising after a run of transparency initiatives. "That's the signal of trust returning," he said. "You don't notice it until it's gone."

The Belief Index became the moral infrastructure of the firm— the heartbeat beneath its new systems. It was imperfect, easily mocked, and entirely transformative. It reminded everyone that culture wasn't mood. It was how fast the place could move.

# The Contribution Ledger

Money, Bill often said, is just where belief shows up. You can preach purpose but, people still look at the payouts. The Contribution Ledger was his attempt to rewrite that language.

Barney-Hamilton had always rewarded tenure. It was the oldest partnership trick in the book—time served equaled value earned. But in a world moving at the speed of code, time was no longer the right proxy. "We've been rewarding tenure," Bill told the committee. "We should be rewarding contribution."

The Ledger divided contribution into four currencies: client value, innovation, mentorship, culture. Each carried a weight that flexed quarterly. The design was messy by intention; it required conversation. "If the metric doesn't start an argument," Bill said, "it's probably measuring the wrong thing."

At first, partners panicked. Equity, that sacred inheritance, was suddenly conditional on behavior. But within months, something strange happened: the resentment faded, replaced by curiosity. Partners began mentoring again—not for optics but for ownership. Analysts started submitting process improvements. Culture, once an afterthought, became an investment category.

Tracy called it "capitalism with guardrails." Bill called it a way to give courage a line item.

*People take risks when they own the outcomes. If you want people to take risks, make them owners of the results.*

The Ledger had its critics, but it changed the firm's metabolism. It made contribution visible. And once people saw it, they started caring about it. In the quarterly partner meetings, numbers weren't enough anymore; people wanted stories. Who had taught? Who had built something worth keeping? Who had renewed a client relationship no one thought savable?

Bill knew he had done something right when he heard a partner say, "My Ledger score's lower this quarter—but my team's belief is higher." That was the sound of culture shifting gears.

# From Design Shops to Judgment Studios: Evolving the Art of Collective Intelligence

In the 1990s, innovation evangelists Max and Gail Taylor created something extraordinary — an ecosystem for accelerated learning and collaboration known as the Accelerated Solutions Environments (ASEs), and fast-paced, grueling transformation events, called Design Shops. These were not normal workshops. They were built for speed and pressure, and for collaboration that forced people to work together.

The Taylors' approach combined visual thinking, systems mapping, and real-time synthesis to unlock what traditional meeting rooms could not: shared ownership. Every voice mattered, every idea was visible, and progress happened through co-creation rather than presentation. The author had the privilege of using this model dozens of times as a consulting partner, watching teams break through cynicism, surface ideas people didn't know they had, and get whole organizations moving again.

The Judgment Studios within Barney-Hamilton represent an AI-era evolution of those same principles. The room is no longer just filled with paper and markers; it now hums with algorithmic partners. Agentic AI systems: tools like Erebus and the firm's own VERITY, replace static whiteboards with living data maps. Yet the spirit is unchanged: gather the right people and focus their attention, then enable them to think together faster than bureaucracy can react.

Where the Design Shops democratized voice, the Judgment Studios democratize intelligence. The ASEs were about drawing out the tacit knowledge in people's heads. The Studios added the firm's curated Memory on top of that. Together, they form a bridge between two eras of problem solving: the analog age of facilitated creativity and the digital age of augmented judgment.

What the Taylors taught us remains timeless: collaboration is not the opposite of speed; it is the engine of it. In the AI era, that lesson matters more than ever. The tools have changed. The tempo has changed. But the heart of transformation: people thinking together, courageously and without hierarchy, remains the same.

In time, the firm would distill the essence of this evolution into a simple construct: the value of AI equals the quality of its data, the precision of its questions, the integrity of its intent, and the judgment of its interpreters. That formula, like the Design Shops before it, reminded them that intelligence gains worth only when it serves wisdom.

# Reflections on AI and Judgment

Bill Ellis believed that the second revolution of intelligence would not belong to machines but to the humans who remembered what thinking felt like before the noise. He often wrote that wisdom doesn't scale. Judgment, might.

In his final notebook entry before retiring for the second time, he wrote,

> *Erebus taught us speed. VERITY taught us reflection. Judgment will teach us balance.*

He had come to see artificial intelligence not as competition but as catalyst, a mirror held to the way we think, or fail to. "Machines," he said, "don't ruin our thinking. They just show how mechanical it already was." The firms that feared AI were the ones that had forgotten how to learn.

For Bill, judgment was not just decision-making; it was moral architecture. It asked not only "What works?" but "What should?" The firms that survived the coming decade would be those that could teach their algorithms empathy—not by coding emotion, but by curating experience.

He wrote,

*Public data teaches prediction. Curated memory teaches understanding. The first tells you what's possible; the second tells you what's right.*

Erebus showed the limits of imitation. VERITY showed the possibilities of something closer to self-awareness. Together they formed the scaffolding for a new kind of intelligence—one that thought with both head and conscience.

In his last entry, dated the night before his final address to the partnership, he wrote:

*We have built something extraordinary—not because it thinks faster, but because it remembers why thinking matters. The next era won't be about AI replacing people; it will be about people becoming more fully human because of AI. The machine is the echo. Judgment is the voice.*

# ACKNOWLEDGMENTS

I am deeply grateful to my friend, Amy Cohn, for her painstaking review of my manuscript, completed while nursing a stress fracture in her foot and traveling between New England and Ann Arbor to visit family. I should have known better than to ask a university professor, one married to a professional writer at that, to perform this task. Or, at a minimum, I should have anticipated a mark-up that resembled the heavily redlined essay returned to a wary freshman by their English 100 professor. Amy's suggestions challenged me to strengthen my arguments and improved the novel immeasurably.

Kudos as well go to Matt and Gail Taylor, whose pioneering work in creating the Accelerated Solutions Environments (ASEs) and Design Shops reshaped how organizations learn, create, and decide. Their ideas inspired the design of Barney-Hamilton's Lab and Judgment Studio—modern reflections of their belief that progress comes from people thinking together with discipline, imagination, and shared purpose.

I also wish to acknowledge several individuals whose names and roles appear in this story. Listed alphabetically by last name, they are:

- o **Thomas F. Frist, Jr.** – Co-founder HCA Healthcare

- o **Jim Harbaugh**, formerly the J. Ira and Nicki Harris Family Head Football Coach at the University of Michigan.
- o **Keith Jackson**, legendary broadcaster
- o **James Earl Jones,** American actor, University of Michigan alumnus
- o **Dusty May**, David and Meridith Kaplan Men's Basketball Coach at the University of Michigan.
- o **Bo Schembechler**, former head football coach at the University of Michigan
- o **Warde Manuel**, Donald R. Shepard Director of Athletics at the University of Michigan.

www.ingramcontent.com/pod-product-compliance
Lightning Source LLC
Chambersburg PA
CBHW060033210326
41520CB00009B/1115